WILL THE BOAT SINK THE WATER?

WILL THE BOAT SINK THE WATER?

The Life of China's Peasants

CHEN GUIDI AND WU CHUNTAO
TRANSLATED FROM CHINESE BY ZHU HONG

PublicAffairs
New York

Published in the United States by PublicAffairs™,
a member of the Perseus Books Group.

PublicAffairs books are available at special discounts for
bulk purchases in the U.S. by corporations, institutions,
and other organizations. For more information, please
contact the Special Markets Department at the Perseus
Books Group, 11 Cambridge Center, Cambridge, MA
02142, call (617) 252–5298, or email
special.markets@perseusbooks.com.

Book Design by Janet Tingey

Library of Congress Cataloging-in-Publication data
Chen, Guidi.
[Zhongguo nong min diao cha. English]
Will the boat sink the water?: the life of China's peasants
    / Chen Guidi and Wu Chuntao; translated by Zhu
    Hong.
p.   cm.
Includes index.
ISBN–13: 978–1–58648–358–6
ISBN–10: 1–58648–358–7
1.   Peasantry—China. 2. China—Rural conditions. 3.
    Rural development—China. I. Chun, Tao. II. Title.
HD1537.C5 C47313
305.5'6330951—dc22
2005055344

First Edition

10 9 8 7 6 5 4 3 2 1

Water holds up the boat;
water may also sink the boat.

Emperor Taizong
(600–649, Tang Dynasty)

CONTENTS

AUTHORS' PREFACE

In 2001, we began our work on our reportage entitled *The Life of China's Peasants* (*Zhongguo Nongmin Diaocha*). Though we had discussed the idea for over ten years, it was when Wu was giving birth to our son in Hefei that we realized we must not put it off any longer: we witnessed a peasant woman dying in childbirth. She died because the family was too poor to afford proper medical attention during the birth.

We traveled to over fifty villages and towns throughout Anhui Province, made several trips to Beijing to talk with authorities, and interviewed thousands of peasants. All of our savings went into writing and publishing the book. *The Life of Chinese Peasants* is an exposé on the inequality and injustice forced upon the Chinese peasantry, who number about 900 million. Our book described the vicious circle that ensnares the peasants of China, where unjust taxes and arbitrary actions—or total inaction—sometimes lead to extreme violence against the peasants.

After more than three long and challenging years, our book of literary reportage, *The Life of China's Peasants*, was completed. A shortened version—about 200,000 characters instead of 320,000—appeared in the November 2003 issue of the literary magazine *Our Times* (*Dangdai*), and the issue sold out within a week. Spreading with the speed of a prairie fire, this version appeared on websites at home and abroad. To this day, many readers still mistake it for the complete book.

One month later, in December 2003, the full version was published and distributed by the People's Literature Publishing House. With its title plainly set down in six block characters across a yellow background, the book's appearance was unprepossessing, to say the least, but even so it took the Beijing Book Fair by storm, and orders for 60,000 copies were taken in just three days. The first print run of 100,000 copies was sold out within a month. For a work of nonfiction—a reportage on a subject that could hardly be considered trendy—it was a phenomenal success, even by the standards of such an established house as the People's Literature Publishing House.

Professor Wang Damin of the Chinese Department of Anhui University described how "readers devoured it avidly, discussed it earnestly; media publicity spread like waves of the sea; literary circles were inspired to impassioned rhetoric." Professor Damin also noted that "the corridors of power were quiet and unperturbed," apparently registering no response to the report.

We later realized that the latter observation was rash. In just one month the book sold over 150,000 copies before suddenly being taken off bookstore shelves by Chinese authorities in March 2004. After that, only pirated editions could be found on the streets, 7 million of which were sold throughout China.

Meanwhile, the media response was truly unprecedented. Producers of all the important talk shows, such as *Face to Face*, *Tell It As It Is*, the popular Spring Festival special, and other programs of China Central Television, which beams to millions of viewers, invited us to appear with them. The Central Broadcasting Company reported on the book at length during its prime-time program. Within two months, from the end of

2003 to the beginning of 2004, we were interviewed by over a hundred reporters from newspapers, magazines, TV, and radio stations as well as websites from across the country. Critical articles appeared in the press and we received a cascade of letters from readers.

The publication of *The Life of China's Peasants* has been compared to a clap of thunder. The publicity blitz following its publication has been compared to shock waves generated by the clap of thunder.

We were totally taken by surprise by this level of public attention. We had assumed that the onslaught of commercialism would mean that works of literature could no longer impact society to any significant extent, not to mention cause a sensation. Of course our book was not exactly "literary" in the strict sense of the word. The deputy editor of the *Beijing Evening News*, Mr. Yan Liqiang, summed up *The Life of China's Peasants* tactfully, saying, "The fact is, when writing on this subject, no one . . . can be simultaneously literary and analytical. It is a feat to . . . master this weighty, complex, and sensitive material to the extent that [the authors] did. The text abounds with signs of [their] struggle to come to grips with the subject matter."

The impact of *The Life of the Chinese Peasants* on mainland China is due not to its literary value but to the fact that it has brought out the stark reality of rural China. It has taken on a complex of problems that is generally referred to as the Triple-Agri (*San-Nong*): the problem of agriculture, the problem of the rural areas, and the problem of the peasant.

In the last analysis, the Triple-Agri is nothing less than the problem of China. Not exclusively an agricultural issue nor an economic one, it is the greatest problem facing the ruling party of China today. The problem is staring us in the face. But over the years, all we got from the media were glowing reports of "happily ever after." City people know as much about the peasants as they know about the man in the moon. The impact of our book came from telling the plain truth about the lives of China's peasants, which inspired in readers from all walks of life not only shock but also heartfelt empathy with the dispossessed.

As our work on the book was drawing to a close, we conducted some studies on readers' responses and were confident that if the manuscript could just get published and hit bookstores' shelves, it would not go unnoticed. And this was because of the nature of our book. As the critic He Xilai said in his introduction to the original book, "This is not a book of good news, even less is it a book glossing over bad news. This book places stark reality in front of the reader without mincing words. This book brings out the Triple-Agri problem in all its complexity, its urgency, its gravity, and its latent danger."

The facts narrated herein are almost without exception garnered from the fearsome "forbidden areas" of writing and journalism, including major criminal cases in rural areas, cases that have alarmed the Communist Party Central Committee but about which the public has been kept in the dark. We disclosed for the first time the obstacles and inside stories relating to the government's push for a new tax and agricultural policy, called "fees for taxes." And we didn't mince words about who is involved: all the players—from the secretary-general of the Communist Party Central Committee to the premier of the State Council (the central government) to the various heads of ministries to officials at the provincial, municipal, county, and township levels all the way down to ordinary peasants in the villages—all are named.

This was unprecedented for writers and readers alike, living as we all do on the Chinese mainland, which has yet to get used to freedom of speech.

Despite the obvious interest in our book, being plunged into a media frenzy did not make us happy. Knowing China only too well and being familiar with the way things are, we actually felt uneasy. Our apprehensions were justified: barely two months after its publication and in the midst of the publicity blitz, *The Life of China's Peasants* was banned by order of the Propaganda Department of the Central Committee and disappeared from bookstores. All references to the book disappeared overnight. It was as if it had never been written, as if the publicity surrounding it had been a dream. For us the shock of the overnight coup was overwhelming; it seemed unreal, like living a nightmare.

To this day we cannot understand where the book went wrong; no one has ever explained to us the reason for the ban. Under pressure from all sides, we had no choice but to remain silent. To our surprise, millions of pirated copies made their way into the hands of readers across the length and breadth of the country, and that was a consolation of sorts. What's more, a number of substantive articles about the book were published. That was another source of encouragement. Dang Guoyin, a noted scholar from the Chinese Academy of Social Sciences, wrote:

A hundred years hence, our descendants will not understand the age we live in. But we have indeed lived through such times, times when you need courage to tell the truth, times when you run a risk to tell the truth, times when people yearned to hear the truth and yet it was hard to get to hear the truth because truth was drowned out by the babble of complacent platitudes. It is precisely for this reason that we are grateful to the couple Chen Guidi and Wu Chuntao for writing this book.

In fact, the truth was being stifled while lies flourished. Following the ban, Zhang Xide, an official named in our investigation, showed up and sued us, saying that our account of the Baimiao Township incident described in "The Long Road" (chapter 4) was libelous. Following the accusation, a local court took up Zhang Xide's case and turned it into a political indictment of the book and its authors.

Corruption within the legal system is a long-standing problem; once caught in the system's coils you are done for. But our readers supported us and that encouraged us. Besides, it was questionable whether the description of the Baimiao Township incident could be construed as libel. Obviously, this supposed libel had nothing to do with the banning of the book. Openness is the best antidote to corruption, we decided, and we assumed that the journalists who had supported us so far would not remain silent and would report on the progress of the suit, which we were sure we would win. At the request of leading members of the Communist Party Committee of Hefei, where we live, who appealed to our sense of patriotism, we promised not to grant any interviews to the foreign press.

But one day we suddenly realized that the media had been muzzled concerning our case. More in sorrow than in anger we asked ourselves, what has happened to the much-vaunted "rule of law"? The media blackout meant that the progress of the lawsuit would not be exposed to the scrutiny of public opinion. Our readers were also denied the right to information about the case. The mainland media were silent. No one stood up for us.

With our backs against the wall, we had no choice but to break our promise and began to grant interviews to foreign journalists, so that the world would know the facts. Actually, we were merely exercising our rights within the framework of the Constitution. Besides, we truly felt that an open China should not be a silent China. Lu Xun, the doyen of modern Chinese letters, has said that only the voice of truth could move the people of China and of the world, that only through the genuine voice of the truth could the Chinese people live side by side with the rest of the world's people.

As of October 2005 the uproar over the libel suit has quieted down, and all that is needed is to wait patiently for the verdict of the court. We fought the suit long and hard, and the facts were made public, that is in itself a victory. The court proceedings ended more than a year ago, but we are still waiting for a verdict. We can only speculate as to what is going on beyond the public gaze. During the waiting period, a new Party secretary of Anhui province, Guo Jinlong, denounced us during an interview with a Hong Kong TV station. He publicly criticized the book as a very bad one that twisted facts and brought bad reputation to the people of Anhui. Not long after that, people started throwing rocks at our home. The attack continued for more than twenty days. No one came to investigate, even though we repeatedly asked the local public security for help. Then, Chen Guidi was asked to resign from his job.

Yet at the same time, other things were encouraging. We received the Lettre Ulysses Award for the Art of Reportage; we were named as Leaders at the Forefront of Change in Asia by *Business Week*; and we were given the title of Asia Hero by *Time* magazine in October 2005.

After the book was banned in China, we were embraced wherever we went by all walks of people, especially peasants. The Chinese central government is working on the "Triple-Agri" problems more than ever. That's partly due to our efforts. But whatever awaits us in the days ahead, we will never regret having spoken up for the peasants of China. We have given voice to the voiceless.

Chen Guidi
Wu Chuntao
March 2006
Anhui Province

INTRODUCTION

BY JOHN POMFRET

current West Coast Correspondent and
former Beijing Bureau Chief for the *Washington Post*

When I was going to university at the end of the 1970s, we were taught that China's Communist Revolution was on the whole a good thing for China's peasants, who comprise the bulk of that country's population. In classes on Chinese history, anthropology and economics, we were told that the Communists came to power and redistributed land to many millions of landless farmers, breaking the backs of the parasitic landlord class. The Communists got rid of opium smoking and illiteracy, my professors enthused, and despite millions of executions and the deaths of 30 million to starvation during the Great Leap Forward, the party truly represented the wishes of China's dispossessed. A revolution is not a dinner party, one of my professors remarked, quoting China's leader, Mao Zedong. Many of us, newly-minted college kids from elite schools and good families, nodded in agreement.

Will the Boat Sink the Water? challenges every assumption of the generally accepted Chinese narrative in the United States—a received wisdom that continues for the most part unchanged and unchallenged since the 1970s. Readers of this work, arguably the most important book to have come out of China in years, cannot help but conclude that China's revolution from the outset was a disaster for the vast majority of China's people. For that reason alone, it should be essential reading for anyone interested in what life was—and is—really like in the People's Republic of China.

Chen and Wu's book on China's peasants was published in China in January 2004 at the end of a short period of relative press and publishing freedom in China. During those years, a series of Chinese historians and social scientists published works that amounted to one of the most significant challenges to the accepted historical narrative in China. Social critics lambasted China's moral vacuum—heresy in a country that prides itself on its ancient culture and supposed traditional values. Economists bemoaned a widening gap between rich and poor that easily surpasses that of the United States—again sacrilege in a place still nominally communist. Historians laid siege to the great symbol of China's revolution—Chairman Mao—showing how his particular brand of cruelty helped fashion China's peculiarly successful brand of totalitarianism, dissecting his debauchery and detailing his sadism, the famines he caused and the lives he destroyed. Chen and Wu's book fell neatly into this tradition. And like many of its counterparts, within two months of publication, it was banned. But not before hundreds of thousands of official copies and millions more pirated editions had been sold.

Chen and Wu's life after the appearance of their best-seller is sadly typical of the fate of many other gutsy Chinese writers. First, one of the characters in their book, an allegedly corrupt apparatchik named Zhang Xide, sued them for defamation. Zhang brought the case in the same county where he had been the county boss. Naturally, given his ties into the party structure there, he won the case; it is currently on appeal. In December 2004, the head of Anhui Province's Communist Party committee blasted Chen and Wu's book for "smearing Anhui province," marking the first time that a Communist official had publicly commented on the book even though the party had already banned it. Within short order, an Anhui newspaper that had been serializing Chen and Wu's next work—on a rarity in China, an uncorrupt judge—pulled the plug on that work. That same day, a gang of thugs pelted Chen and Wu's two-room apartment with bricks, forcing them to flee Anhui's capital of Hefei with their son. The police told them there was nothing they could do. Chen was also asked to resign from his work unit—the Anhui Writer's Union. When last contacted, they were living in a small village in the poor, southeastern province of Jiangxi. It was not immediately clear if they were doing research there or hiding from goon squads, whom party officials now routinely hire to muzzle and even kill their enemies—perceived or otherwise.

Chen and Wu's book stands as a challenge to another, more recent, narrative—one about China's rise. There is a lot of talk these days that China is going to become the world's next great superpower. From the Pentagon to Wall Street, China's emergence as a global power is viewed with a titillating combination of fear and excitement. In recent years, a series of books have been published in the West predicting everything from an imminent war with China to China's ultimate surpassing of America as the world's next economic giant. The hype about China is breathless and unrelenting.

Will the Boat Sink the Water? is an important antidote to the boosterish pablum churned out by many China experts these days. It is a street-level look at the downside, and the dark side, of China's economic juggernaut. In this book, you will meet a cast of characters that has generally been denied a voice in the worldwide frenzy accompanied by China's rise. Their stories are important ones, amounting to China's version of Jacob Riis' 1890 classic about poverty in America, *How the Other Half Lives.*

Chen and Wu's book also helps us to put current Communist policy in perspective. During his annual state-of-the nation address to China's rubber-stamp parliament in March 2006, China's prime minister, Wen Jiabao, set out what he dubbed as a "major historic task." The aim, he said, was to close the gap between China's dirt-poor countryside and its booming cities. Wen pledged to abolish all rural taxes and increase spending on rural social services and education as China creates what he called "a new socialist countryside."

Spooked by a restive countryside, a rapid rise in the number of demonstrations and riots by China's peasants, the Chinese Communist Party is saying it cares about the countryside. Leaders like Wen and president Hu Jintao routinely commit themselves to bettering the lot of China's dispossessed. Hu even went down one of China's many perilous mine shafts to share a New Year's supper with miners. But while Wen and Hu's remonstrations have been portrayed as something new in the Western press and particularly by China boosters, readers of *Will the Boat Sink The Water?* will understand that they are nothing new. China's Communists have been saying that they cared about the peasantry ever since they rode to power on their backs in 1949. But at every turn, as Chen and Wu show, they have let them down.

In 1993, Chen and Wu write, China's legislature vowed to limit taxes to 5 percent of peasants' income, but within one year taxes and fees were forcing China's peasants into debt. A decade before that, the government committed itself to devoting 18 percent of its budget toward rural services. But it has never come even close; in 2005 it devoted only 9 percent. Meanwhile, the ranks of China's bureaucracy, most of them laboring in the countryside, have ballooned, jumping from 2.2 million in 1979 to well over 10 million today. Premier Wen did not say how they would be supported now that the peasants don't have to pay any more taxes. But the logical conclusion of anyone familiar with Chen and Wu's work is that when push comes to shove, the peasants are going to have to pay.

Chen and Wu set their book in their home province of Anhui. American readers might be familiar with Anhui because it was here that Nobel prize winning author Pearl Buck set her most famous work, *The Good Earth*—the story of a poverty-stricken Chinese family. Anhui is one of China's poorest provinces. Indeed, for years after most other parts of China were opened to Western travelers, foreigners were banned from Anhui because the Communist government did not want them to see the widespread misery there. Anhui was the site of a series of ethically questionable genetic research projects led by Harvard University researchers in the early years of the twenty-first century. The researchers promised impoverished farmers—desperate for health care—free medical check-ups and medical treatment in exchange for blood samples. The only problem was that once the researchers pulled the blood, they essentially left town.

Husband and wife, Chen and Wu have collaborated before— on a report on pollution on the Huai River, China's sixth longest waterway and arguably its dirtiest. They visited 48 cities along the Huai and reported that of the river's 191 large tributaries, 80 percent of the water had turned black. Pollutants expelled into the river from various factories bonded together into enormous barge-like collections of scum that putrefied the river. At times the brown lather—a noxious mix of trash, effluent, and untreated waste—stretched more than 60 miles and stood six feet high in places. Local residents wore masks and wet towels across their faces to keep from retching. Drinking water had so damaged the health of those who lived along the river that the People's Liberation Army stopped conscripting local residents because they were unfit for service.

Chen's "Warning of the Huai River" proves to be a cautionary tale of life in the People's Republic of China. Just as Premier

Wen did in March 2006 with China's peasants, the government promised to tackle the pollution problem. Teams were sent to the Huai River to shut down polluting factories, just like teams have been sent from Beijing to ensure that peasants are no longer being forced to pay taxes and illegal fees. Within two years, however, 40 percent of the polluting plants had re-opened. And by 2004, when I traveled the river and met with Chen and Wu in their Anhui home, all the firms were back in operation, without pollution controls. Because of an electricity shortage, local governments had shut down smokestack scrubbers and waste-water treatment facilities. That July, another 60-mile carpet of sludge swept down the river, killing millions of fish and devastating wildlife. Could the same fate be awaiting China's farmers?

Near the end of *Will the Boat Sink the Water?* Chen and Wu write about a group of corrupt village leaders who spend their days using tax revenues to fill their bellies. The party appa-ratchiks' feasting prompts Chen and Wu to conclude that, contrary to what my professors taught me, perhaps the revolution *is* a dinner party. Only one where the peasants have never been given a seat at the table.

Los Angeles
March 15, 2006

POST-LIBERATION TIME LINE OF EVENTS IMPORTANT TO CHINESE PEASANTS, WITH EMPHASIS ON AGRICULTURE

1949 Founding of the People's Republic of China (PRC).

1951–53 Korean War.

1952 Land-reform movement.

1954 Passage of the Constitution of the PRC.

1955 Nationalization of industry and trade.

1955–58 Collectivization of agriculture: mutual-help teams—agricultural cooperative—commune.

1955 Campaign against the Hufeng antirevolutionary clique.

1956 Hundred Flowers movement, Mao's call for all to "bloom and contend."

1957 "Anti-rightist movement," suppressing those who had "bloomed and contended."

1958 Great Leap Forward.

1959 "Antirightist deviation" campaign.

1959–62 The Great Famine; deaths estimated at over 30 million.

1963 The then head of state, Liu Shaoqi, restores rights of peasants to have a private family plot.

1964 Socialist education campaign in the countryside.

1965 Campaign against the play *Hairei Dismissed by the Emperor* (prelude to the Cultural Revolution).

1966–76 Cultural Revolution.

1969 (September) The Ninth National Party Congress: Lin Biao is confirmed as Mao's heir and the Cultural Revolution is legitimized.

1976 (January) Death of Premier Zhou Enlai.

1976 The Tangshan earthquake.

1976 (September) Death of Mao Zedong.

1976 (October) Gang of Four arrested.

1978 (December) At the Eleventh National Party Congress, Deng Xiaoping announces the new policy of "Reform and Open Up," and make plans for China's modernization, under the new slogan "Emancipate our minds; seek truth from facts."

1978 A handful of peasants in Xiaogang Village, Fengyang County, Anhui, take out land contracts for independent farming. From then onward, experiments in reforming the agricultural system by "household contracts" are carried out in many areas in Anhui.

1982 (January) The Politbureau of the Party Central Committee passes the Number 1 Document, approving the household-contract system.

1982 (February) The Twelfth Party Congress; Hu Yaobang becomes general secretary of the Communist Party.

1984 (October) The Third Plenary Session of the Twelfth Party Congress announces the reform of the economic system, with emphasis on urban areas.

1989 Tiananmen Square incident.

1990 Deng Xiaoping tours parts of South China and reiterates the policy of Reform and Open Up.

1993 The Plenary Session of the Eighth National People's Congress confirms the household-contract system, which has been introduced in parts of the countryside.

1993 Trial launch of the "reform of the tax and fees system" in rural areas with the aim of reducing the peasants' financial burden. Items on the agenda include standardizing rural taxation, regulating fees and charges, reducing or eliminating charges for governmental and educational projects, eliminating conscripted labor and other items, and writing these changes into law.

1993 (December) The State Council (central government) announces plans for reform of the financial system.

1996 (December) The "Number 13 Circular" announces the decision of the Party Central Committee and the State Council to reduce the peasants' burden.

1997 (July 1) Hong Kong is returned to China.

1998 (March) The Party Central and the State Council announces "rules for the conscription [state purchase] of grain," to protect peasants' interests.

1999 Ninth National People's Congress: Premier Zhu Rongji formally announces a project to reform the system of rural taxes and charges, in order to reduce the peasants' burden. The reform, called "tax for fees" for short, is first tried out in Anhui Province.

2000 Li Changping writes a letter to Premier Zhu Rongji, deploring the condition of the peasants, stating: "The peasant's life is so hard, the countryside is so poor, agriculture is in such a dangerous condition." This statement is later referred to as the *san-nong wenti*, the "three-peasant problem," called here the Triple-Agri. (This is a recent Chinese coinage: *nongmin* = "peasant"; *nongcun* = countryside"; *nong ye* = "agriculture")

2001 (February) The "tax for fees" project is tried out nationwide.

I

THE MARTYR

Restlessness in the Village

Sometimes the unmistakable line between life and death is blurred: a person may be dead and gone and yet remain among the living. At least that seemed to be the case with Ding Zuoming.

Ding Zuoming is dead. His death would probably not be reckoned as "weightier than Mount Tai,"* but on February 10, 2000—a full eight years after his death—when we asked around for the way to Luying Village, we were invariably greeted by the question "Looking for Ding Zuoming's place?"

Ding Zuoming was an ordinary peasant of Luying Village within the jurisdiction of Jiwangchang Township in Lixin County, a notoriously poverty-stricken backwater in Anhui province on the flatlands north of the Huai River. If there was something different about Ding Zuoming, it was that he had a few more years of schooling than others—he actually graduated

---

*Mount Tai, in Shandong Province, is one of the largest, most scenic, and culturally most significant mountains in China. A center of spirituality for centuries, it also symbolizes the spirit of the nation. The expression "weightier than Mount Tai" means that a person's death has meaning—for example, it was for a good cause.

from senior high. He was an exceptionally good student. When there was no food on the table, he would go and bury his head in the water jar, fill himself up with cold water and go cheerfully to school. During the national exams for college entrance, he scored just a few marks below the entrance margin. If he had not been a native of Lixin County—if he had been born in Beijing or Shanghai—he would have been a college student right away, for his grades exceeded the entrance requirements there. Actually, if he had been born anywhere but Luying Village, he would have had a different fate. But being only a graduate of the local high school, he had no choice but to go back to his native village, and thus he ended up as a dirt-poor peasant like any other, going down to the fields every day to tend to the crops. But Ding, having a little more book learning than other peasants, liked to leaf through the newspapers and listen to radio broadcasts, and was somewhat literal-minded. In short, he had a mind of his own. He was modest to a fault in his dealings with people. But he would stick to the letter of the law, was not afraid to call a spade a spade, and had the temerity to stand up to the cadres and speak to them as equals. This led to more trouble for him than was the lot of an ordinary peasant. Eventually it cost him his life.

Ding Zuoming had died long ago. Why did the people in Lixin County still refer to "Ding Zuoming's place"? Was there a road that would lead us to him?

The morning of February 20, 1993, Ding Zuoming and seven other villagers who had lodged complaints to the county authorities about the conduct of village affairs were unexpectedly invited to the township office to attend a meeting. At the meeting, the township leaders announced that the county leadership at the next higher level, to whom they had previously made appeals, were concerned about their grievances, and that now Ding Zuoming and his group should elect two men from among themselves, to be joined by two Party members and two cadres from their village, and the six would form a work group to audit the books of Luying Village the very next day. Ding and his fellow villagers were jubilant, their despondency forgotten. Back home, some actually went to the village store to get fire-crackers, hoping to dispel their pent-up resentment with a few loud bangs. But the Spring Festival was just over and the stores were sold out. So the next day, February 21, when he got an unexpected summons from the township security, Ding walked out of his home with a light step, never dreaming that it would be the most fateful day of his life.

But we are getting ahead of ourselves.

Lixin County was a new county created after the Liberation, in 1949, when the Communists took over the Chinese mainland. Before that, the area had been in a spot where six different counties converged, and was consequently overlooked by all six jurisdictions. It was a poor area, inundated with yellow mud when it rained, which made roads impassable, not to mention the pervasive alkaline soil dotted with many sandy patches. Luying Village was a godforsaken hole to begin with, and after the disastrous flood of 1991, the people were bled bone-dry.

Our story begins in early 1993, with the upcoming Spring Festival, which would fall on January 23—just around the corner. But there was no sign of coming festivities. There is a tra-ditional Chinese saying, "Rich or poor, home for New Year," but many migrant laborers could not return home for the Spring Festival—something unheard of. But now they dared not show their faces, for they were unable to pay the exorbitant fees and taxes waiting for them. By year's end (according to the lunar calendar), the annual per capita income was under 400 yuan, or about US$50 ($1 is roughly 8 yuan), but taxes and other payments imposed from above such as "village cash reserves" amounted to 103.17 yuan per head. After twelve months' back-breaking work in the fields, all that the villagers could hope to keep back from the tax collectors was their grain rations; everything else would have to go toward paying taxes and other charges, including so-called reserves—monies kept back for "community projects." Households that had had a bad harvest did not even make enough to pay off the taxes, not to mention the reserves. The head of local security, who was working hand in glove with the village Party bosses, stated, "Pay up, or you'll find yourself behind bars."

During this time Ding Zuoming had been doing something that no one else in his village had ever dared contemplate. He spent several nights putting together all the information he had culled from the papers and radio broadcasts regarding the Party's new policies laid down at the recently convened (1993) National Agricultural Conference in Beijing, information that he now compressed into a short, simple, easily understood list of important points, and went around the village spreading the word. He worked clandestinely, reminiscent of the Communist underground in the Nationalist-controlled areas during the old days before the Liberation. It made him anxious, yet it was exhilarating when he saw people's eyes sparkle in the light of a murky light bulb hanging from the ceiling as Ding assured them, "These excessive 'reserves' are decidedly against the Party Central Committee's directions."*

The peasants, used to being kicked around, had always trusted Ding for his learning and good sense. Now, at one of their informal get-togethers, again the villagers were impressed and

*The Central Committee of the Communist Party of China. Often called simply the Central Committee or the Party Central (*dang zhong yang*). For more information on the Party Central Committee, see http://en.wikipedia.org/wiki/ Central_Committee_of_the_Communist_Party_ of_China.

gave their tacit approval of his activities as he continued to spread the word. But they still couldn't help wondering about where this could lead, saying, "Look at all the villages around us, look at the neighboring townships. Aren't the bosses doing the same thing? Heaven is high and the emperor beyond our reach. What can you do about it?"

But Ding was not intimidated. "Might is not always right."

Ding read to them word for word the latest regulation spelled out by the State Council (the central government): agricultural taxes may not exceed 5 percent of annual per capita income from the previous year.* Ding emphasized the 5 percent limit, saying, "It's obvious, our village is making us pay more than five times the limit. This most recent National Agricultural Conference requested that leadership at all levels protect the peasants and lighten their burden. Our bosses around here are way out of order. Let's hear what the township leadership has to say."

Some of the villagers still had reservations. "Will the township bother to listen to us?"

A newly demobilized army man couldn't help raising his voice: "'Officials oppress and the people revolt'—an old saying. Anyway, we are going by the rules in appealing to the leadership. If the township ignores us, we can go higher up, to the county!"

The mood of the gathering warmed up as the discussion continued. One said that the village Party boss, Dong Yingfu, had rented out the granary built with funds raised by the community

---

*The State Council is the central government of the People's Republic of China and is the chief civilian administrative body of the PRC. It is chaired by the premier and its approximately fifty members are the heads of each governmental department and agency. The State Council is often called simply the central government, in newspaper reports and also in these pages. Detailed information on the State Council is available at http://en.wikipedia.org/wiki/State_Council_of_the_People's_Republic_of_China.

and pocketed more than 9,000 yuan through the transaction. Later he got rid of the granary altogether and pocketed 30,000 to 40,000 in cash. What's worse, another pointed out, was that during the last flood, this same Dong had kept back food and clothing designated for their village, even though Party directives had warned that embezzling flood relief could cost you your head. Moreover, some added, the fines for violations of the one-child policy and other "reserves" extracted from the peasants were either not recorded or the records were intentionally messed up.*

The focus of talk moved one tier up, from the village to the township leaders. One thing led to another, and the villagers' resentment grew from a simmer to a boil. According to some of those present, Kang Zichang, the head of the township, had a rascal of a son who would run amok in the villages sporting an electric prodder and a pair of handcuffs, extorting money right and left under the pretext of collecting taxes. Even during the flood disaster, when there were express directives against any taxation of the peasants, this puppy of Township Head Kang still committed daylight robbery. With a few members of the militia in tow, he had once descended on the village like the Japanese occupying army of the hateful past. The villagers who shut their doors on Kang's gang had their doors broken down and even got a bill for the "labor" involved. Their pockets filled to bulging, the thugs swaggered into a restaurant, enjoyed an orgy of feasting and drinking, then charged the bill to an "expense account!" The villagers got worked up as more revelations surfaced. Finally, they turned to Ding Zuoming for a decision as to what action to take.

"To make an accusation you need evidence," Ding said.

---

*The government started encouraging the practice of the one-child policy in 1979. It is enforced unevenly, depending on the location (stricter enforcement in urban areas) and the particular ethnic population.

"Let's go to the township Party Committee and demand a general audit of the village books."

And so, Ding Zuoming with seven others went to the township office and told the township Party boss, Li Kunfu, of their concerns and requested an audit of the village books. Li read through the list of "reserves" exacted by the village leaders and said, "Yes indeed, this is excessive. We will look through it and let you know in a day or two."

Two days passed and nothing happened. Another two days passed, followed by another three. Then, at a meeting called by the township where the various village cadres were present, including those from Luying Village, Ren Kaicai, the township deputy Party boss in charge of policy and legal affairs, called on the Party boss of Luying Village, Dong Yingfu, to clarify the question of excessive taxes. Dong was furious—everybody was doing the same—why single him out? When he learned that the villagers had appealed to the township leadership and had requested an audit, he suspected that people were jealous of his newly built tile-roof house. He spat out a challenge: "Some people want to audit my records. Some even want to tear down my house! I'd like to meet the son-of-a-bitch who has the gall! Others say that I cannot afford to buy a tractor and build a tile-roof house on my salary alone. Cannot afford to? But I did, and what can you do about it? It is called being smart. Too bad you are miserably poor! Serves you right! Want to pick a fight? I guess you're tired of living."

Everyone present was shocked that a mere village cadre could have such an outburst at his township superior, but Ren let it pass. When word trickled down to Luying Village about Dong's outburst at the meeting, everyone was outraged. "What! Is there no law under the Communist sky?"

*   *   *

Ding Zuoming was not going to let the issue go away. Three days before Spring Festival, he wrote out a complete list of the excessive taxes and "village cash reserves" imposed on the peasants of Luying Village and personally took it a further step up the official ladder—to the Disciplinary Committee of the Lixin County Party Committee.

The officer at the reception desk pointed out that Spring Festival was right around the corner, and that Ding Zuoming would have to wait to present his document.

Spring Festival was very sober at Luying Village; there were barely any sounds of festivities.

The days dragged on and soon it was February 9, the eighteenth day of the first lunar month. Spring Festival had come and gone, and still there was no response from the county's Party Disciplinary Committee. People went to look up Ding and discovered that he had spent the whole of the Spring Festival holiday writing out a second letter of complaint against the leadership at Luying Village, listing in detail the heavy burden of the peasants under the abuses of the village as well as the township bosses, describing in detail how they violated Party policy and fleeced the people.

All were moved by the spirit of Ding Zuoming. Indeed, if nobody dares to stick his neck out, what hope is there for us as a nation? That very same night of February 9, the villagers made a collection, one yuan here, eighty fen there, and under cover of night they sent off eight men, including Ding Zuoming, as their representatives, to head for the county seat of Lixin.

The head of the county's general office who received the representatives saw the letter and realized that the situation in Luying Village was more serious than they had imagined. He immediately reported to the Lixin County Party secretary, Dai Wenhu. Dai, newly arrived at his post, was quite firm in his support. "We will direct the township to set up an auditing group as soon as possible, to go over the financial records of Luying Village. As to the problem of the township leadership, we will look into that, too."

Ding and his seven companions did not linger in the county seat after presenting the letter; to save expenses, they boarded the bus and headed home. Despite the rough ride in the bus, they couldn't help savoring Dai's words of support, not knowing that disaster and death were waiting for them at the other end.

Tragedy in the Township

On February 11, the twentieth day of the lunar New Year, that is, two days after Ding and company's visit to the county seat, at about half past three in the afternoon, two villagers were soaking in the last of the winter sun playing "six rounds," a locally invented rustic form of chess. The deputy village chief,* Ding Yanle, happened to pass by. He stopped in his tracks when he saw Ding Zuoming among the group of onlookers. By now Deputy Village Chief Ding Yanle knew that Ding's letter of complaint had included information on himself and his wife, Sun, accusing them of embezzling money from the "village cash reserve" and the fines paid for violations of the one-child policy. Ding Yanle had been storing up resentment and was spoiling for a fight.

He started with a threat. "Hey, this is gambling, I can have you arrested," he said to the two players, but he kept his eyes on Ding Zuoming.

Ding Zuoming couldn't help remarking in surprise, "But this

*The head of the village committee and his deputy are village administrators; Party functionaries are not responsible for village administration. They are parallel hierarchies.

is just a game. Even if there is any arresting to do, it's up to the local security."

"Don't be so sure!" retorted Ding Yanle fiercely.

Ding Zuoming had always despised those creatures that put on a swagger the minute they are in power. He was not at all impressed by Ding Yanle's boast, but seeing that the fellow was trying to pick a fight, he kept silent.

Ding Yanle, getting no response, started to shove Ding Zuoming, saying, "What! You want to fight! Come on, come on!"

Ding never imagined that a deputy village chief would stoop so low. He started to walk away, but Ding Yanle followed hard on his heels, and attempted to shove Ding with his shoulder. Ding Zuoming hastily backed off, the shove fell short of the mark, and Ding Yanle landed in the field near by. Now at last Ding Yanle found the excuse that he was looking for.

Of course Ding Zuoming knew that he had ruffled a few feathers in high places, and had expected retaliation sooner or later. But the lowdown trick that he had just witnessed was beneath contempt, and he walked away in disgust.

As expected, the matter was not over for Ding Yanle. Later the same afternoon, he went six times to the home of Ding Zuoming howling for revenge, claiming that the latter had beaten him up. Ding Zuoming's wife, having no idea what had happened, kept apologizing, but Ding Yanle would have none of it. One of his sons even brought a meat cleaver to Ding Zuoming's home and shouted threats.

That same night of February 11, the villagers persuaded Ding Zuoming to leave home for a while. Ding was not one to be intimidated by bullying, but he considered the situation: When he and the other men went to present their petition to the county two days before, on February 9, the newly installed county Party head, Dai Wenhu, had promised to order the audit that they had petitioned for, so it was just a matter of time. Not wishing to divert attention from the main issue, Ding swallowed his pride and left Luying Village at dawn the next morning. Predictably, just at dawn Ding Yanle brought his whole family to Ding Zuoming's place, out for his blood. Not finding him, Ding Yanle left, proclaiming, "Yesterday Ding Zuoming wounded me with his blows. I need to go to the hospital!" The village Party boss, Dong Yingfu, who had lain low throughout all the commotion, now made a show of helping take Ding Yanle to the hospital.

At that point, Ding Yanle's wife, Sun, who ran the village family-planning program, went to the head of the township, Kang Zichang, and the deputy Party boss, Ren Kaicai, and handed in a formal accusation against Ding Zuoming: her husband, Ding Yanle, "had implemented the one-child policy overzealously and had offended Ding Zuoming, who stopped him on a village path and beat him up."

Kang and Ren were more than happy to see this trumped-up charge against Ding Zuoming. They had already received a firm order from their superiors at the county to form a working group to check the financial records of Luying Village, an order that, obviously, reflected badly on their own leadership. The group must include those who had made the complaints. It was obvious to Kang and Ren that Ding Zuoming was the ringleader who had brought matters to a head. Kang and Ren lost no time in directing the township security force to take action on the accusation against Ding Zuoming. And the township security, being a tool of the township bosses, in turn wasted not a moment before sending out a notice for Ding Zuoming to report to their office immediately.

By the time Ding Zuoming received the summons on the fateful morning of February 21, he had not only come out of hiding but had on the previous morning been invited to attend a meeting at the township, where the word was out that the auditing should start the very next day. Ding was perplexed by the summons from the township security. He could only surmise that it was Ding Yanle up to one of his tricks again. But Ding felt sure that once the audit got going, all the abuses in Luying Village would be brought to light. As for himself, Ding had nothing to hide. He walked out of the house and made for the township security office with a light step, which is where our story first started.

What happened inside the security office on the day of February 21 after Ding Zuoming walked in was never made public, but after the case was closed, there was an internal report, which we were able to acquire for this investigation.

According to this report, the minute Ding Zuoming stepped into the office, the deputy chief of township security, Peng Zhizhong, barked at him, "How dare you attack Ding Yanle?"

"I never attacked him, I've never attacked anyone!" Ding protested.

The accusation and the denial were repeated back and forth over and over again. Peng's logic was "If you did not attack Ding Yanle, why would his wife make those accusations to the township?" Ding Zuoming replied, "If anyone present at the scene that day, even a child, testified that I attacked Ding Yanle, I would take the consequences."

Peng lost patience and pronounced sentence: "One, you must pay 280.50 yuan for Ding Yanle's medical bills. Two, you must use a cart to fetch Ding Yanle back from the hospital on a township market day."

Of course Ding Zuoming would not accept the preposterous sentence. He had picked up some knowledge of legal procedures from his constant reading of newspapers, and he said, "I never attacked Ding Yanle. I can appeal your sentence."

Peng was enraged. He pointed his finger at Ding Zuoming and shouted, "I can have you arrested this very minute!"

Ding replied, "Even if your 'sentence' can stand, mine is not a criminal offense. And even if you hold me in detention, you must give a reason for detention within twenty-four hours."

Peng retorted, "Good, I will detain you for twenty-three-and-a-half-hours. After that, if you refuse to pay up, I will detain you for another twenty-three-and-a-half-hours. This will go on until you pay." At this, he called to three security hirelings, Zhu Chuanji, Ji Hongli, and Zhao Jinxi, and told them to take Ding to the "detention cell." The government had passed clear-cut rules forbidding the local security from setting up such cells.

Against Ding Zuoming's protests, Peng said to the three men, "The lout has no manners. Too spirited. Soften him up a bit." Then he retired.

The three men knew what was meant by "softening up." One of the men present, Zhu, had been Ding's classmate in high school and now sneaked out to avoid a personal confrontation. But he knew that Boss Peng would never be satisfied unless they could break Ding, so before leaving, he suggested that the other two try the "horse's walk," one of their cruelest forms of torture.

Ji and Zhao dragged Ding Zuoming from the cell into an unused reception room to do the "horse's walk."* Of course Ding resisted. Despite having spent twelve years in school, Ding was no pale scholar. Having been toughened by years of farm work, he was more than a handful for Ji and Zhao, who could hardly subdue him, not to mention doing the horse's walk. Just then another security man, Wang Jinjun, came in with a club. Ji and Zhao clamored that Ding Zuoming was attacking them, so

*The "horse's walk" is a local invention on which no specific information is available.

Wang raised his club and struck Ding right and left. Ding tried to defend himself, but was hit repeatedly on the arms and the back. Although he was groaning in pain, he would not give in. Ding resisted the "horse's walk," and Wang beat him mercilessly with the club. When the club split, he kicked Ding and used an electric prodder to get him to a kneeling position. When Wang, exhausted, stopped the beating, Ji picked up the stump of a broken shoulder pole* and continued where Wang had left off.

By now Ding Zuoming had stopped moaning. He was filled with shock and fear when he realized that as long as he did not "soften up," these thugs would kill him. But he still would not give in. Glaring at Ji, Zhao, and Wang, he shouted at the top of his voice, "True, I accused the village cadres. They are bleeding the peasants. It's against Party policy. Kill me, but I won't give in. If you kill me, my ghost will haunt you all!" Ji looked up and met Ding Zuoming's bloodshot eyes and the piece of wood slipped from his hand. This enraged Wang, who screamed hysterically, "You spineless bastard! Afraid of him! How dare he talk big in this place!" Goaded, Ji picked up the stump and went after Ding again. Meanwhile Zhao took a dirty rag and stuffed Ding's mouth. The three men continued hitting Ding for another twenty minutes.

By chance, the political director of the township security was home on sick leave; he was alerted about the commotion in his domain and came to interfere, putting a stop to the violence.

*A shoulder pole is a length of wood or bamboo five or six feet long that is balanced across the shoulders and is still used by Chinese villagers today to carry anything and everything: from sacks of grain to baskets of produce or piglets bound for market—even small children.

A Case That Caught the Eye
of the Party Central Committee

When some villagers, including members of the auditing group, found Ding Zuoming, the latter was nearly dead. They sobbed as they bent over his prostrate body, knowing that Ding had been brought to this terrible state because he had championed their cause. Some ran to tell his family. Old Ding, his father, rushed in and stumbled to his knees at the sight of his son. By now Ding Zuoming's face was clammy and deathly pale, and his trembling lips could hardly utter a word.

Meanwhile, the deputy head of the township security, Peng Zhizhong, sauntered in to check if Ding Zuoming had been "softened up." When the old father realized that the new arrival was a leader around the place and that his son had been beaten for refusing to pay up, he turned to beg Peng, "I will apologize to Ding Yanle, I promise to pay his medical bills! Please let my son go!"

Actually, Peng Zhizhong himself was somewhat shocked that his men had gone so far. Seeing Ding Zuoming's condition, he was more than happy to accommodate the old father's plea and let them go. He waved them away, but flung a warning at their retreating backs: "Let's get this clear, the payment must be on my table by tomorrow."

Old Ding, helped by the villagers, rushed his son to the township hospital. Ding Zuoming was suffering severe pain in the abdomen and the township hospital sent him on to the county hospital. There he was diagnosed with a ruptured spleen and given blood transfusions, but it was too late. The next morning, the day after the village audit that he had agitated for was supposed to start, Ding Zuoming died on the operating table.

Ding's father was prostrate with grief. "My son, you poor simpleton! You are in the right, but they have might. Don't you know that the leg is always stronger than the arm?"

Ding's wife could not accept the reality of what had happened, wailing, "How could you let them kill you over two hundred yuan! Isn't your life more precious! How are we to live, with two sick old parents and three small children!"

The villagers tried to console them, but they were also saddened. How could Ding Zuoming, so smart and resourceful, let himself be beaten to death without calling for help.

The news that Ding Zuoming had been killed for speaking up for everybody hit the area like a thunder bolt.

The peasants of Luying Village had had enough. Rage swept away their timidity. They left their houses and marched up to the home of Ding Yanle, whose provocation had started the trouble. By then, Ding Yanle, having gotten word that trouble was brewing, had snuck out of the hospital and made off with his family. He has never been heard of since. Eight years have passed. It was rumored that the family had been spotted in Shanghai, then in Nanjing, and even as far off as Hainan.

Drawing a blank at Ding Yanle's, the crowd headed for the township security office, but by then the high and mighty Peng Zhizhong and his thugs had also made themselves scarce.

Thwarted now for a second time, the enraged villagers decided to go straight to the Lixin County seat. They raised clouds of dust as they moved forward to the accompaniment of the hoots and toots of tractors and flat-bed tricycles and trucks and carts trundling along the road. As they passed through the neighboring villages, more people joined them, and together the angry crowd made its way to the county seat. Obviously, Luying Village was not the only village where the peasants found it hard to make a living. The problems that Ding had presented to the county leaders, the demand to audit the books, actually reflected the common aspirations of them all. And so they could not stand by and see Ding Zuoming beaten to death for his efforts and do nothing about it. Their unspoken understanding was: if we don't band together and do something now, we could suffer the same fate as Ding Zuoming. Eventually, the group that set out from Luying Village snowballed into a crowd of three thousand before they arrived at the county seat.

The "Ding Zuoming affair" that took place in the security office of Jiwangchang Township of Lixin County of Anhui Province on February 21, 1993, and ended in Ding's death the next day will never be forgotten. A man gave up his young life to protest the peasants' excessive burden; his death called national attention to the condition of the Chinese peasants.

Officials of the Lixin County Party Committee and the county government rushed out to meet the crowd halfway down the road, fearful that the situation would spiral out of control. They acknowledged the facts, and tried to handle the problem fairly. What the authorities wanted to avoid above all was that news of the events would get out to the general public, so they banned any reporting on the affair.

The news did leak out after all, not to the provincial authorities, as the county officials had feared, but, worse, straight to the Party Central Committee and the State Council.

The person behind this leak was Kong Xiangying, a reporter for the Anhui branch of the Xinhua News Agency. Kong was in charge of reporting on agricultural affairs in the province. When he heard of the story of Ding Zuoming he saw it as a mirror that reflected a multitude of issues in rural China. And the timing was good. The fact that the tragedy had occurred when the problem of the peasants' excessive tax burden was a top concern at the Party Central Committee made the story stand out even more starkly. Here was an educated young peasant who had reported on precisely this issue, had even gotten the support of the county, and he had been killed in broad daylight—beaten to death while in the custody of the township security force. Kong's sense of civic duty and mission led him to drop everything and go to Jiwangchang Township to do his own investigation. Less constrained by the gag order than local people, he quickly wrote up a report covering the facts, which he sent straight to the Xinhua main office in Beijing. The main office immediately published Kong's story, unabridged, in *Domestic Trends*, an internal publication meant exclusively for the eyes of the top leadership.

One day, a staff member at the General Office of the Anhui provincial government got the shock of his life when he picked up the phone. On the line was Chen Junsheng, secretary-general of the General Office of the State Council in Beijing. Chen Junsheng got straight to the point: "We have learned that Ding Zuoming, a young peasant of Luying Village, Lixin County, in your province, has been persecuted to death for reporting on the excessive burden of the peasants. How did the provincial leadership deal with this case?" No answer. The provincial government had heard nothing from the county or the prefecture about Ding Zuoming, and naturally had no answer.*

Secretary-General Chen continued, "Let me know how the case is being handled. Leaders at the Party Central Committee have taken notice and jotted down directives. Call me as soon as you have information." The secretary-general left numbers not only for his office phone and home phone, but also for the emergency "red phone" within Zhongnanhai, the Party Central Committee headquarters, in Beijing, which faces Tiananmen Square. Nothing like that had ever happened in the history of the Anhui provincial government. The officer immediately reported to his bosses, the provincial leaders, and then set about wiring directives down to the prefecture and county levels.

The Party secretary of Lixin County, Dai Wenhu, who had earlier on listened to the complaints of the peasants with Ding Zuoming at their head and had ordered the audit, now realized

*China's system of administrative units, as described throughout the story: Central, province, municipal (prefectural), county, township, and village.

the gravity of the situation. If it was established that Ding's death was linked to the problem of "excessive burden of the peasants," everyone would be in the hot seat, from the village to the township all the way to the county, and Dai Wenhu himself, though newly appointed to the position of county Party secretary, could not avoid being tainted. After thinking over all sides of the case, Dai chose the path of least resistance—to gloss over the whole affair. And so within twenty-four hours of getting the call, the county Party and government leadership sent off a report to their superiors at the provincial government in which they stated that Ding Zuoming's death was the result of a personal dispute pure and simple that was totally unrelated to the problem of the "peasants' excessive burden."

When Dai Wenhu decided to slant the report as he did, he was ignorant of the fact that recently a thousand peasants had mounted a protest against excessive burdens in Renshou County, Sichuan Province, and that the protesters had clashed with the police and burned one police car. This explained the central government's current anxiety over events in Anhui. Dai, unaware of this background, never imagined that in trying to be clever and glossing over the problem, he was actually killing his own political future.

Lixin County's report was exactly the kind that the provincial Party and government leaders wanted to see, and they promptly wired the gist of the report to Chen Junsheng in Beijing.

Secretary-General Chen of the General Office of the State Council was a careful man. Seeing the discrepancy between this report and the earlier Xinhua News Agency's internal report, he realized that what was at stake was not so much the *handling* of the case as the *nature* of the case: Was it really a civil dispute, or was it revenge taken on the peasants for reporting on their excessive burden? Chen followed up with the Xinhua News Agency, which stood by its own story. But in the interests of thoroughness, they relayed Secretary-General Chen's query to their branch office in Anhui. When the writer of the original report, Kong, saw the query regarding the discrepancy between the two stories, he of course stood by his own version. To clarify the problem once and for all, the Anhui branch office of Xinhua requested that the Party and government dispatch an investigation team down to the village to clear up the problem on-site.

A joint investigation team was quickly formed, with members from the Disciplinary Committee of the Party Central Committee, the Legal Bureau of the State Council, the State Planning Commission, the Ministry of Agriculture, and the Supreme People's Procuratorate.* They did not involve the provincial or local authorities, but left Beijing and headed straight for Luying Village. The local governments at various levels were in total shock when they realized what was happening right under their noses.

The investigation team first offered condolences to Ding Zuoming's family and then started meeting with the villagers. The investigation did not limit itself to Luying, but took in two neighboring villages as well. Local cadres were not invited to participate in the interviews, and the peasants the team interviewed were put under protection. News of the investigation spread, and peasants from more distant villages came over to talk to the investigation team. In no time at all, the news spread that a living "Judge Bao"** in plain clothes has arrived from the capital and was in their midst.

*The people's procuratorates are state organs for legal supervision. The Supreme People's Procuratorate is the highest procuratorial organ. It reports to and is supervised by the National People's Congress and its Standing Committee. For further information, see http://english.people.com.cn/data/organs/procuratorate.html, accessed November 26, 2005.

**Judge Bao was a judge of the Song Dynasty (960–1279) whose name became a byword for legal integrity.

The Tears of the Joint Investigation Team Members

Seven years later, on the afternoon of October 30, 2000, in an office in the Anhui provincial government building in Hefei, we met with Wu Zhaoren, who had been deputy head of the provincial Agricultural Economic Committee for seventeen years. Now retired, he was a consultant to the provincial government of Anhui and chairman of the Agricultural Economics Association. He started talking about the events surrounding the activities of the joint investigation team. It was as if everything had happened the day before. He had accompanied the joint investigation team back to Beijing by accident, he explained, because he himself was on a business trip to Beijing. But he did not hide the fact that his bosses at the Anhui provincial government were very curious to know what the investigation team had found out in Luying Village and what views they had formed. Wu said that even today he could remember the names of two members of the team who were from the Ministry of Agriculture: Li Xiangang, head of the Department for Supervising the Peasants' Burdens, which was an administrative unit of the Bureau for the Supervision and Direction of the Agricultural Economy, and his deputy, Huang Wei. Huang Wei, Wu remarked, was a very capable female comrade, and Li Xiangang had once been secretary to the deputy minister, Jiang Chunyun. The fact that Li and his deputy, Huang, were both included in the investigation team shows how seriously the Central Committee took the case. The head of the team was Zeng Xiaodong, head of the Central Committee's Supervisory Committee for Law Enforcement.

Wu told us that Zeng Xiaodong, in describing to him the condition of the peasants of Lixin County, had said tearfully, shaking his head, "I never dreamed that so many years after Liberation, the peasants are still so poor, their lives so hard, their tax burden so heavy, and they are so badly treated by cadres."

What impressed Wu most from the team members' account was that the reality was much worse than the situation described in Ding Zuoming's original report. Apart from the bosses, who had tile-roof houses, all of the peasants lived in hovels. The village was so desperately poor that in some production teams, people survived by selling their blood at regular intervals. Even so, the taxes and fines kept piling on. The investigation team established beyond a doubt that Ding Zuoming was a thorn in the side of the leadership, not because of his violation of the one-child policy, but because he had reported on the excessive burdens imposed on the peasants. And for that, Ding was beaten to death. As he said this, Zeng's lips trembled and tears rolled down his cheeks.

Other members of the investigation told Wu that the moment they arrived in the village, some of the older peasants fell down on their knees, supplicating for justice. It was heart-wrenching. Just think, if they had not been weighed down by grief unprecedented in their long lives, if not for their extreme feelings of oppression, how could these venerable elders have overcome their sense of humiliation and gone down on both knees in supplication to people who were their grandsons' age? Weren't these peasants the kind of people that we usually refer to as having reversed their fate under Communism—*fanshen*—and become the masters of the country?

The case of Ding Zuoming's beating and death for reporting on the peasants' excessive burdens had been taken most seriously by the Central Committee. Twenty-six days after his death, on March 19, 1993, the General Office of the Communist Party Central Committee and the General Office of the State Council issued, jointly, "Emergency Directives Regarding Relieving the Peasants' Burden." On June 20, the State Council convened a meeting in Beijing on the issue of relieving the peasants' burden. One month later, on July 22, the two general offices again issued an emergency directive, confirming regulations regarding agricultural products to be taxed. Altogether, 122 agricultural products were declared exempt, making illegal any forced taxation under one pretext or another. The directive also listed items that should be exempt or should be subject to deferred payment of taxes, or where the regulations should be revised. It was unprecedented in the forty-four-year history of the People's Republic of China for so many emergency directives regarding the peasants' burden to be issued in such a short time—not to mention the national conference that was convened on the subject.

Charges were brought, and the Intermediate Court of Fuyang Prefecture, one level above county level, tried the case in open court in Lixin County. On trial were seven men who were directly involved in the death of Ding Zuoming. The club-wielding Wang Jinjun was given the death sentence and was stripped of all political rights. As to the other thugs, Zhao Jinxi was sentenced to life imprisonment, and Ji Hongli got fifteen years. The deputy head of the security office, Peng Zhizhong, who had ordered the "softening up," was sentenced to twelve years in prison, and Zhu Chuanji, Ding's former classmate who had suggested the "horse's walk" torture and then had snuck away, was sentenced to seven years in prison.

The Party Committee and government body of Fuyang Prefecture took disciplinary action against Party and administrative cadres on the county and township levels who had been involved in the case: Dai Wenhu, the head of the Party in Lixin County, was given a warning; Xu Huaitang, the deputy head of the county government, was demoted. Li Kunfu, the Party head of Jiwangchang township, received a severe warning; Kang Zichang, the head of the Jiwangchang township government, was put on probation as a Party member and was stripped of all Party and administrative positions; Ren Kaicai, the township deputy Party boss, was removed from his position.

A happy ending indeed! Or was it?

* * *

On an early spring day in February of 2000 we walked into Ding Zuoming's former home. It was obvious that the family, having lost its mainstay, was finding it hard to get by, even though they had been exempt from taxes since Ding's death. The old father's tears still flowed at the mention of past events. He showed us the formal verdict of the prefectural court, which stipulated that the family was entitled to payment of damages. Over the years they had made endless inquiries at the prefecture office and had paid the exorbitant fee for "implementation of the court order," but by the time of our visit, no money had been paid to them. Ding's mother was a bedridden invalid. Ding's widow had broken her right arm hauling fertilizer; she was incapacitated, and could do only light work. The three children were exempt from tuition, but the two eldest, fourteen and twelve, had left school to help around the house.

Leaving Luying Village, we went to visit Ding Zuoming's grave. Silently we stood before the grave marker, hoping that such a tragedy would not be repeated.

We had hoped that Ding Zuoming, the first martyr to the cause of protecting the peasants' rights, would be the last. But we found that in another village of another township of another county, a similar tragedy had occurred—this time bloodier, more shocking, and on a larger scale.

2

THE VILLAGE TYRANT

Four Killed in a Matter of Minutes

With the swelling tide of commercialism, the number eight, *ba*, has been growing in favor, as in Chinese, its pronunciation rhymes with the term *fa*, "to make it."

Under normal circumstances, the date February 18, 1998, which includes two eights, would be considered an auspicious date. But in Zhang Village, Tangnan Township, Guzhen County, Anhui Province, that date would be forever remembered as a day of mourning.

Zhang Village was situated in the lowlands on the banks of the Huai River. Prone to droughts to begin with, and burdened by the village leaders' excessive fines and taxes, the people dragged out their days from one year's end to another. This is not to say that everyone in the village took things lying down. For instance, there were four men with backbone—Zhang Jiaquan, Zhang Jiayu, Zhang Hongchuan, and Zhang Guimao—who had repeatedly gone to the village cadres and the township Party committee to demand an audit of the village finances.

One of the village officials, Deputy Village Chief Zhang Guiquan, was seething in anger and gnashing his teeth at the unending stream of complaints and accusations, which he knew targeted him, among others; he was accused of embezzling public funds. But with backing at the township level, Deputy Village Chief Zhang could afford to snap his fingers at the villagers, whom he treated as dirt anyway. As to the villagers, they steered clear of him, knowing that he was totally unscrupulous when the chips were down.

One day, Deputy Village Chief Zhang summoned over to his home two members of the township security force. Then he sent word to Zhang Hongchuan, one of the hotheads who had been making accusations against him, to come over so that they could go over the village finances together. Zhang, not suspecting any mischief and conscious that right was on his side, was not at all intimidated by the prospect of facing Deputy Village Chief Zhang Guiquan. He went over cheerfully, expecting to do some checking of the books. But the minute he stepped into the deputy village chief's house, the two township security flunkies and two of Zhang Guiquan's own sons sprang on him and pounded him to within an inch of his life. If not for the poor man's nephew, who was alerted and ran to his uncle's rescue, it was hard to say what would have been left of Zhang Hongchuan after the attack.

This show of violence on the part of Zhang Guiquan was meant as a preliminary warning, but instead of intimidating the villagers it only served to mobilize them. Veteran village cadres, Party members, and the eighty-seven households of the village banded together and went twice to the township office and five times to the home of the village Party head, Zhang Dianfeng, to demand an inquiry into Deputy Village Chief Zhang's outrageous behavior and to conduct an audit of the village books.

Badgered by these repeated appeals, the Party apparatus of Tangnan Township finally decided that something must be done. Just then it happened that their superiors at Guzhen County directed all the townships to conduct a general audit of the villages under their own supervision. The township Party head, Zuo Peiyu, announced to some of the peasants from Zhang Village, who happened to be there, presenting another of their petitions, "What luck! The county is launching a general auditing, and we have decided to start with your village! The head of our township's Party disciplinary committee, Comrade Wang, will lead a work team, including three accountants from the township financial office. They will be heading for your village right away."

This news threw Zhang Village into a fever of excitement.

On February 9, led by Wang and three accountants and reinforced with the addition of Xue, a township officer in charge of supervising Zhang Village, the work team deployed in the village to carry out their mission.

On the same day, with Wang presiding, the eighty-seven households held earnest consultations and elected twelve representatives from among themselves to join the work team to conduct an auditing of the village books. Among the twelve selected were Zhang Hongchuan, who had already suffered an attack at the hands of Deputy Village Chief Zhang Guiquan, and three others who had always championed peasants' rights—Zhang Jiayu, Zhang Guiyu, and Zhang Guimao—were among the twelve elected. Knowing Deputy Village Chief Zhang Guiquan through and through for the kind of bully he was, the group did not expect things to go smoothly. They laid out strict rules and guidelines for conducting the auditing. Moreover, as a precaution, the twelve representatives made a private pact that in case Deputy Village Chief Zhang Guiquan got tough with any one of them, the rest would rally around whoever it was, to prevent anything untoward from happening.

As expected, Deputy Village Chief Zhang Guiquan reached into his bag of tricks to throw dust into people's eyes to obstruct the auditing. For instance, he spread rumors that someone had tried to poison one of his sons. When all his tricks failed, he swore publicly during a meeting of the village cadres, "Twelve fucking representatives, actually trying to check on me! They must be dreaming! Even if they do get rid of me, their own lives will be over. If they are lucky enough to come out alive, I'll make them lose an arm or a leg at the very least!"

On February 14, the audit group decided to go through the record of the "village cash reserves." The village deputy Party boss, Zhang Dianhu, who was in charge of finances, tried to fob the group off by turning over some obsolete records. This was really a ploy to cover up for Zhang Guiquan, but the latter, in his mad rage, could not tell friend from foe and started abusing his colleague, blaming him for digging up old scores. On February 15, Deputy Village Chief Zhang Guiquan's daughter-in-law put out the word that her father-in-law was itching to stick a knife into someone. Neither the township nor the village leadership paid attention to these warnings. The work group, too, thought it was just more of Zhang Guiquan's bluster. Nobody imagined that on the morning of February 18, nine days after the start of the auditing, Deputy Village Chief Zhang would actually launch a killing spree.

February 18 fell on the twenty-second day of the first month in the lunar calendar, and this meant that rain was expected the next day, but a light spring shower arrived early. Starting the previous night, the rain pattered on and on with no sign of letting up. When February 18 dawned, most of the villagers were still curled up in their bedrolls.

Fifty-eight-year-old Wei Surong, however, was already up and busying herself at the stove. Although she did not involve herself in public affairs as her husband did, she knew exactly what was going on in the village. Her husband, Zhang Guiyu, was one of the twelve representatives charged with the auditing and he had been carrying out his task every day, rain or shine.

Obviously their fellow villagers trusted her husband, as the auditing closely concerned the interests of the community. Wei Surong knew it wouldn't do to let her husband be late for work, so she got out of bed early every morning to get his breakfast ready.

The spring rain was still pattering away, and a gray mist hung outside the window. Wei Surong set the table, and her husband and their son, Pine, sat down to eat. The clock's hands pointed to ten minutes past seven. Just then Deputy Village Chief Zhang Guiquan showed up at their doorstep, followed by his sons number five, Zhang Yuliang, and number seven, Zhang Leyi, and the village accountant, Zhang Jiahui and his son, Zhang Jie, right behind them.*

Deputy Village Chief Zhang's showing up at that hour with two of his sons and the accountant, who was obviously hostile to the auditing, was a clear sign that he was bent on mischief. The only thing missing was an excuse to act. The village accountant's son, naturally displeased by the auditing of his father's books, began by taunting Zhang Guiyu: "Well, what have you dug up? Do we get a share of the spoils?"

Zhang Guiyu got the drift of the group's intentions. He got up from the table and said coldly, "The people have chosen me for the audit. How can I refuse?"

At this, Deputy Village Chief Zhang's son number seven broke in with an obscenity: "Mother-fucker! Who are you to audit anything?!"

Zhang Guiyu was shocked at the language of the young man, who was a generation younger than he. He retorted, "How dare you? Would you use the same language to your own father?"

The father broke in, saying, "Curse you! It's no more than

---

*Since all the sons were knife-wielding adults, they would have been born before the one-child policy came into force. But, cadres were often able to violate the policy with impunity.

what you deserve!" as he signaled to his two sons to let him have it.

The attack came so suddenly that Zhang Guiyu was stunned for a moment, unable to take in the situation. His wife, Wei Surong, rushed over and tried to drag him into the inner room, shouting at Deputy Village Chief Zhang, "How dare you crash into our own home to attack us! What do you want, anyway?"

Meanwhile, son number seven picked up a club leaning against the door, and son number five picked up a scythe lying on the floor. The accountant held Zhang Guiyu by the waist while son number seven sprang forward with the club to hit him. Zhang Guiyu managed to struggle out of the accountant's grip and, seeing that they were out for his blood, picked up a brick on the floor. Wei Surong picked up a kitchen knife lying on the stove top, ready to defend herself.

The two sides faced each other; the situation was explosive.

The commotion alarmed the neighbors. The two sons of Deputy Village Chief Zhang, seeing that they were outnumbered, snuck out of the house.

But Deputy Village Chief Zhang was not about to give up. He walked toward the back of the house, throwing a challenge to Zhang Guiyu: "Come on, meet me over there, if you have the balls!"

Zhang Guiyu, an upstanding man who had never taken a challenge lying down, was certainly not going to cave in to a village cadre's bullying. He followed Zhang to the back of the house, saying, "You know it is the township's order for a general audit. The people chose me. Am I to blame? You'd better put a lock on that mouth of yours. I am going to check your books and dig out the problems! And what can you do about it?"

Deputy Village Chief Zhang had secretly signaled son number seven to go home for reinforcements. Now he came back with his two brothers, son number one, Zhang Jiachi, and son number six, Zhang Chaowei, both of them carrying hidden weapons. Son number six started hitting Zhang Giuyu the moment he arrived, while son number five struck the brick out of Zhang Guiyu's hand. Seeing that the disarmed Zhang Guiyu was not giving up and still fighting, son number six took out a dagger he had stuck in his rubber boots and a meat cleaver that was hidden under his jacket. Brandishing these weapons, he struck Zhang Guiyu on the head and stabbed him in the chest. Taken by surprise, Zhang Guiyu fell heavily to the ground, without uttering a sound.

By then other members of the work group, Zhang Hongchuan and Zhang Guimao, both rushed over, honoring their previous agreement to stick together in an emergency. They were shocked when they saw Zhang Guiyu lying on the ground covered in his own blood, and cursed Deputy Village Chief Zhang and screamed for a doctor.

By now, Deputy Village Chief Zhang had completely lost his senses. Seeing Zhang Hongchuan and Zhang Guimao at the scene, he said with a sinister smile, "Damn it, you are just on time. I've been waiting for you!" Turning to son number one, he shouted, "Kill! Kill! Twelve bastards trying to check my books, kill them all!"

Son number five, who happened to be standing closest to Zhang Hongchuan, sprang on him immediately, stabbing him in the chest, the abdomen, and the hips. Zhang Hongchuan stopped breathing before he could put up any resistance.

Just as son number five was attacking Zhang Hongchuan, Deputy Village Chief Zhang himself pinned the other village representative, Zhang Guimao, tightly from the back and cursed him: "Fuck your mother! Going around raising complaints against me? Trying to audit my books? Come on and get your fill of auditing!" Though restrained from behind, Zhang Guimao was tall and muscular and still managed to grapple with the deputy village chief. The latter, finding himself no match for his victim, called to son number seven, "Leyi, come and put him down!" Son number seven raised the meat cleaver in his hand and crashed it down on Zhang Guimao's skull. Meanwhile, son number one, who had become delirious at the scene of the carnage, now joined his brother; he straddled Zhang Guimao and stabbed him three times in the back with the butcher's knife. According to forensic evidence gathered later, Zhang Guimao's skull was cracked by five blows to the head, and his left lung was pierced.

Meanwhile Zhang Guiyu, in whose home the attack had first started, was groaning in pain and about to breathe his last. Son number one, seeing that he was still breathing, sprang at him and stabbed him five times in the chest and abdomen.

Thus, in the twinkling of an eye, three members of the auditing group—Zhang Guiyu, Zhang Hongchuan, and Zhang Guimao—were lying dead or dying at the back of Zhang Guiyu's house. The rain pattered on, now mixed with blood on the ground; the sickening smell of blood hung heavy in the air.

Just then, Zhang Guiyu's elder brother, Zhang Guiyue, heard of what had befallen his brother. He hastily snatched up a stick used for stirring cattle feed and rushed over. Yue's eyesight was bad and he did not recognize his brother lying on the ground. Suddenly he found himself face to face with Zhang Guiquan's son number one. "Isn't that my little brother?!" he exclaimed. Before he could finish the sentence, the butcher knife was already lodged in his breast.

In the melee, Zhang Guiyu's sixteen-year-old son, Pine, tried to move his father to take him to hospital. However, son number six aimed his bloody meat cleaver straight at the back of the young fellow's head. Someone let out a gasp, and Pine turned around just in the nick of time to avoid the blow, which landed on his shoulder instead. Pine turned and ran for his life.

Thus, within a matter of minutes, four people were killed and one wounded as the rain fell on Zhang Village.

Deputy Village Chief Zhang Guiquan's son number four, Zhang Simao, rushed over, knife in hand, anxious not to miss his share of the kill. Just then the voice of the village Party boss, Zhang Dianfeng, boomed out over the village P.A. system, calling on the audit group to start their morning's work.

Appointed to Leading Position
While Serving a Sentence

The power of organization is considerable, and can be formidable when combined with political power. The sheer number of Chinese peasants could make them overwhelming, but they are scattered, and have no organizational resources to counter oppression. The rural cadres, on the other hand, are highly organized; they are the legal representatives of state power in the countryside. If this body of representatives puts aside the will of the central government,* the highest authority, which has delegated power to them, and appropriates the organizational resources of the state for their own interests, the consequences will be disastrous.

Deputy Village Chief Zhang Guiquan's education was barely equivalent to primary-school level, but relying on his power as village chief and the power of his clan—he had seven sons—he was able to control Zhang Village and act as the absolute tyrant of the area.

In 1997, he knew perfectly well that the county's figure for the levy of grain tax** was unchanged from the previous year, but he went ahead anyway and imposed an extra fifty jin (1.1 U.S. pound) per head. He had myriad ways to fleece the peas-

* "Central government" refers to the State Council of the People's Republic of China.

**The grain tax—a mandatory amount of grain that the peasant has to sell to the government at a fixed priced—is said to have been established as early as

WILL THE BOAT SINK THE WATER?

ants. One of his inventions was the "five taxes and one fee:" by his order, any family that raised a pig must pay an extra 45 yuan; any family who built a new house had to pay a tax ranging from 150 to 500 yuan (the precise figure to be determined by Zhang's whim of the moment); owners of old houses in the village had to pay 50 yuan; any family that planted peanuts had to pay 10 yuan per *mu* (about 1,660 square meters, or one sixth of a hectare); any family that acquired a tractor must pay a tax of 50 yuan. (Zhang Guiyue, who was killed while trying to save his brother, Zhang Guiyu, had scraped together his savings to acquire a tractor, but had to come up with 45 yuan tax before he ever started up the machine. Now the owner was dead while the brand new tractor stood unused under a shelter.) As for two other inventions of Deputy Village Chief Zhang—the "birth-control" and "child-care" fees—no one could decipher their meaning. The amount of the fines for violations of the one-child policy depended on his whim. Moreover, he would casually issue a piece of paper instead of a regular receipt for payments and he never made a record in the books. On the other hand, he himself never contributed to the village cash-reserve fund, and even less would he pay the "five taxes and one fee" personally invented by himself. In a word, he invented ingenious ways to fleece the peasants.

Relying on his enforcement power, this deputy village chief encroached on public lands; appropriated fish ponds, public property, and public funds to himself. He stopped at nothing. He would not tolerate the slightest sign of discontent on the part of the villagers, not to mention any attempt to defy him. For instance, one day Zhang Chaohua, the wife of a demobilized army veteran, got into a quarrel with him over the allot-

---

the Xia Dynasty, around 2200 B.C. More can be learned about the grain tax in Peter Morris, "China to Abolish Age-Old Grain Tax," *Asia Times*, March 12, 2004 (http://www.atimes.com/atimes/China/FC12Ad03.html, accessed November 27, 2005).

ment of threshing ground.* The woman started arguing with him, while standing on a bridge. To him it was absolutely outrageous that anyone could talk back to him like that, much less a woman. In a fit of anger, Deputy Village Chief Zhang pushed her off the bridge. She lay there unconscious for hours and appeared to be dead. Later she regained consciousness, but she remained paralyzed for life. Her husband dragged Deputy Village Chief Zhang before the Guzhen County Court and the court ruled that Zhang must pay 8,000 yuan to the family for damages. Of course, Deputy Village Chief Zhang refused to pay anything at all. Finally, when the issue came to a head and could not be evaded, Zhang embezzled the sum out of the village public funds.

How could such a villain get to be a leader in the village? Granted, he was only a deputy village chief, but where were the village chief and the Party head? Were they working hand in glove with him, or did they look the other way? It was one of the mysteries that we hoped to solve through our investigation.

The more we learned about Deputy Village Chief Zhang's background, the more preposterous the whole situation appeared. It turned out that the problems in Zhang Village were not limited to shady finances. Organizational irregularities at the grassroots level were extremely alarming. On May 20, 1992, this same Zhang had been convicted of embezzlement and rape and sentenced to one year in prison by the Guzhen County Court, with two years' probation. During the two years' probation period, Zhang Village's administrative area was redistributed and Zhang Guiquan got himself into the position of deputy chief of the newly formed Zhang Village. The vil-

---

*"Threshing ground allotment" refers to the fact that after the agricultural communes were gradually broken up, the land was divided and contracted to individual households. The threshing ground was also divided into sections for individual household use, and there could be disagreements as to how these divisions were undertaken.

lagers complained that no one had elected him to the position, that there never had been any consultation, and that Zhang Guiquan's appointment had been forced on the people by the township Party boss and a few individuals within the village Party organization.

The fact that a criminal and sociopath could actually be appointed by two levels of the Party organization, township and village, to a position of power while still on probation for a court sentence, in effect set him up to commit more atrocities.

The behavior pattern of Zhang Guiquan presents the characteristics of the village bully of traditional Chinese society. But Zhang differed from this traditional figure in many ways. The village bully of old times was a pariah in the community and did not own a great deal of land or property. He certainly did not enjoy any legal authority. Now, however, the likes of Zhang Guiquan could appropriate public land and property with no restrictions because they were legally invested with power over the village. In other words, a village cadre such as Zhang Guiquan was a worse public affliction on the people than the village bullies of the old days.

The case of Zhang Guiquan and his sons killing people in broad daylight, though exceptionally horrific, was not so unique. In our investigation, we discovered that local bullies who lorded it over the peasants was a common phenomenon of village life. Zhang Guiquan being just one of the products of China's peculiar mechanism of power at the rural grassroots level. It is easy to define the problem, but the real question is how to make sure that such a tragedy as that in Zhang Village cannot recur.

A Long-Drawn-Out Suffering

Twenty minutes after getting a call for help, the antiriot police of Guzhen County surrounded Zhang Village. The murder suspects, Zhang Guiquan and his sons, were immediately arrested, except for son number seven, Zhang Leyi, who had fled. According to the testimony of the victims' families and witnesses, Zhang Leyi had put all the murder weapons in a bag and walked away, right in front of the village Party head, Zhang Dianfeng, who did not identify him to the fully armed antiriot police, so he was able to sneak out via a small path behind the house of a villager, Huang, and escape.

News of the murders in Zhang Village spread like wildfire. But both the county and the township authorities totally ignored the fact that the whole affair had been sparked by the peasants' demand for their democratic rights and for a lightening of their burden of taxes. The authorities avoided the subject like poison. The day after the tragic incident, while the whole village was still in shock and mourning, the county cable TV station suddenly announced a news item. According to the TV announcement, an extremely grave case of "manslaughter" arising from "a civic dispute" had occurred in Zhang Village in Tangnan Township. The screen showed pictures of a scythe and kitchen knife as the murder weapons. Of course, the scythe and kitchen knife on display had been taken from the victim Zhang Guiyu's home, since the police could not find any murder weapons, which had been removed from the scene of the crime. The whole report was a farcical fabrication.

As soon as the story aired on TV, Zhang Village exploded in indignation. Members of the victims' families—Zhang Liang, the only son of the murdered Zhang Guimao, and Zhang Guiju, who had lost two brothers, Zhang Guiyu and Zhang Guiyue—and many others were all enraged by the TV broadcast. The very next morning, February 20, they gathered, three hun-

dred–strong, and went to the broadcasting station to demand
an explanation. Why was the incident called "manslaughter?"
What was the so-called "civic dispute" that the victims, representatives elected by the villagers, were supposed to be engaged
in with Deputy Village Chief Zhang Guiquan? The real problem, the villagers said, was that a criminal still serving his sentence had became the deputy village chief and was lording it
over the other villagers. The villagers, groaning under excessive
tax burdens, had demanded an audit of the books, which was
their democratic right. The audit had been ordered by the county
authorities, and was to have been supervised by the township
authorities, but down in the village, people engaged in the
auditing were victims of a barbarous intentional slaughter, not
"manslaughter."

The local TV producer was struck dumb by the questions. He
had never imagined that there were so many sides to the issue,
and that it was a case of premeditated murder. He had no
choice but to confess that he put out the broadcast by order of
the county authorities. The dead cannot be resurrected, true,
but at least there must be a just verdict. The victims had been
killed because they were champions of the peasants and had
been entrusted by the peasants to look after their interests. This
ghastly chain of events was totally unacceptable, and the fabricated TV news item was even more aggravating, adding insult
to extreme injury. The enraged villagers decided to confront the
county Party boss.

The county Party and government headquarters was right
next to the county TV station, separated by a wall. When the
villagers made their way out of the station building, they discovered that the street was filled with people. The news had
spread, and many people had been outraged by the flagrant
atrocity of the killings. When people learned that Zhang Village
had turned out en masse to have it out with the TV station, they
sensed that something was afoot. Nowadays, news reports were

rarely reliable, especially reports of major incidents. And so people poured out into the streets to find out the truth of the matter for themselves. In no time at all, three thousand people were milling around the town of Guzhen.

The county authorities, being right next to the TV station, had a clear picture of the situation. By the time the villagers made their way to their office, the county's Party and government officials had disappeared.

On February 21, the day following their fruitless trip to the county seat, the villagers were notified by the village Party boss, Zhang Dianfeng, to meet in Huang's house at the western end of the village. Huang had built the house for his son's coming marriage. The young man was still working in the city, and the house, standing empty, was often used for meetings and other events.

When the villagers gathered for the meeting, they discovered that leaders from the township had descended upon them. Present were the deputy head of the township, He Jingkuei, and the Party head for legal affairs, Qiu Ya, as well as members from the township security force. It turned out that the reason for their presence was to seal up people's mouths.

The atmosphere at the meeting was extremely tense. He Jingkuei opened the meeting by reading sections of the criminal code, and then announced that it was forbidden to appeal to the higher authorities, or to start a disturbance, or to gossip about the incident. Everyone present was nervous, especially the family members whose loved ones had been killed. They were made to feel as if they had transgressed the law and were now being treated as if they fit into two of the "four pariah" categories of the old days: forbidden to "talk out of turn," and forbidden to "act irresponsibly."* It seemed as if the victims were under suspicion and were being controlled from all sides.

*The four pariahs (*di fu fan huai*) are the landlord, the rich peasant, the counterrevolutionary, and the bad element.

After the meeting, Zhang Guiyu's widow, Wei Surong, collapsed on her bed and sobbed. Her husband had died for nothing, it seemed, and there was nowhere to appeal for justice. She was even forbidden to mention the frightful event. She cried because the ways of the world seemed so dark and inscrutable, and she felt she was about to go mad.

On May 7, nearly three months after the tragedy, a newspaper based in the provincial capital published a story on its second page, titled, "Village Chief's Temper Flares Up; Four Villagers Lose Their Lives." The article was published just when the procurator of the city of Bengbu, which had jurisdiction over the county, was just about to transfer the case to the municipal court, for public prosecution. The article was ingeniously worded to manipulate public opinion as to the nature of the incident, insinuating that it was the result of tempers getting out of hand rather than revenge against the peasant auditors.

It began with a carefully crafted background description: "The deputy village chief was offended by the extremist language of the villagers; supported by his sons he got into a fight with the latter, the incident ending in four deaths."

The reader would easily come to the conclusion that the villagers' extremist language had initially given offense, which led to the deputy chief's explosion of anger, which led to the killings. According to this version of events, the villagers were the troublemakers and those who had been killed had brought about their own deaths.

But a careful reader could not help noticing the gaps between the lines: Since it was a "fight" between two groups, why was it that only people on the villagers' side had died? And why did this deputy village chief want to fight the villagers to the death? What exactly was the "extremist language" used by the villagers? What were the words that infuriated the deputy village chief so that he went on a killing spree? The article did not answer any of these questions, perhaps it could not, or dared not, spell out the truth.

The article completely ignored the plain truth: that the villagers had demanded their democratic rights and refused to bear excessive financial burdens. These important facts were intentionally ignored, and therein lurks a conspiracy. Thus, a conflict that many Chinese would consider a life-and-death struggle between good and evil, civilization and barbarity, progress and regression was distorted into a fistfight in which some foul-mouthed village ruffians ended up dead, and deservedly so.

The people of Zhang Village were once more up in arms. They challenged the publisher of the newspaper: "This is a matter of life and death! How dare you publish that trash without checking the facts!"

But, the editors countered, how could they check into every report that crossed their desks? They explained that they had followed the proper procedures, and that the report carried the official stamp of the public prosecutor's office, which absolved them as editors from the necessity of checking the facts.

The situation was very clear. This atrocity took place in the spring of 1998—not, like the Ding Zuoming case, in 1993. In the meantime, the Party Central Committee had repeatedly issued documents forbidding exacerbating the peasants' burden, and had spelled out the punishments to be meted out to violators of such orders: township Party and government officials would be disciplined if villages under their jurisdiction were overburdened, and the same up the ladder: the county's Party and government officials must submit written self-criticism to their superiors. When the Anhui provincial authorities were informed of those harshly worded directives, they added a rule of their own to demonstrate their determination to implement the Party Central Committee's orders: the Party and government authorities of the relevant cities and prefectures must also submit written self-criticism to them, their provincial superiors.

The documents were timely and the spirit that they promoted was undoubtedly correct. The severe measures toward erring cadres were doubtless genuinely designed to protect the interests of the peasants. But can self-criticism really be counted on to magically solve the problems of cadres at the grass roots?

Zhang Guiquan was not any ordinary deputy village chief of a village; he had become a village cadre while still a convicted criminal on probation. As serious as this was, he not only had increased the peasants' burden but also had committed murder. The Party Central Committee had laid down clear guidelines: cases where peasants' excessive burden led to one death or to more than six peasants' complaining to higher authorities must be reported to the Party Central Committee. Zhang Guiquan and his sons had killed four people and wounded one—hair-raising atrocities. Should such crimes be reported, and if so, then how?

Neither in Guzhen County nor in Bengbu did the leadership want to face the situation squarely. They probably did not lack conscience, but the events were so sudden, so stark, that they were left with no wiggle room. The Ding Zuoming tragedy, which had so shaken the Party Central Committee, was still fresh in people's minds. The kind of responsibility they bore and the kind of risk they ran in dealing with the current case were clear to all cadres. Obviously, none of them wanted to take responsibility or run any risk. How else can we explain all the strange happenings in the aftermath of the affair, much less explain why the loss of four lives—even those of mere peasants— was dealt with so off-handedly?

Of course the people who absolutely could not accept the situation were the families of the victims. Zhang Liang, Wei Surong, and several other family members of the victims plucked up their courage and once again went to the county authorities and had an audience with the county Party head. They dropped to their knees in front of the young Party head, sobbing out their grievances. When they mentioned that their loved ones were tragically killed in the course of checking the village finances, the Party head flew into a temper: "Who said it has anything to do with auditing? The whole county is going through auditing, how come only your people are killed and no one else?"

The family members were stunned, at a loss for words.

By the logic of this Party boss, a young girl who was raped and wanted justice could be told, "The world is full of beautiful young women; how come you and only you are raped?" Such "logic" is outrageous.

The arrests of Zhang Guiquan and his sons did in fact facilitate the auditing of the village finances, and many irregularities of the village's cadres began to surface. Undoubtedly the problems in Zhang Village were not limited to Zhang Guiquan alone: the Party head, the village chief, and the accountant were all implicated. They had feared and opposed the auditing from the beginning. But the general auditing was ordered by the county, and the village auditing group was appointed and approved by the township. Much as they hated and feared the auditing and were on pins and needles all the time, they were not so stupid as to go on a killing spree. Fortunately for these village cadres who were all more or less compromised, they soon sensed that with the passing of time, the county and township leadership themselves had lost interest in the auditing and were trying all they could to gloss over the crimes of the Zhang father and sons. In this kind of atmosphere, the village cadres resumed their defiance as the auditing dragged on.

When the auditing group discovered that in 1997 the peasants of Zhang Village had been overtaxed sixty jin of grain per person, which was obviously against Party policy, they put the case before the village Party boss, Zhang Dianfeng. Zhang, not at all disconcerted, took it all in stride. "Yes," he said, with a grand manner, "it was by my order. I had my reasons for ordering the extra sixty jin per person. You need not concern yourself." The auditing group also found out that four village cadres had stolen 2,600 yuan from the sale of village land and had divided it among themselves, and that the village Party boss, Zhang Dianfeng, had taken 6,000 yuan from the sale for himself. He blandly explained to the auditing group, "I know about this. This is called 'compensation for caretaking.'" When asked whether they had a right to take this money, the Party boss said defiantly, "I had an end in view."

On another occasion, the auditing group asked another village cadre, "The watering fee of 4,000 yuan for our rice paddies had been paid in full, so why was four thousand yuan held back for this same expense from the land-sale revenue?" The man, having no answer, flew into a temper, leaving the auditing at an impasse.

Not long afterward, word got about that the auditing at Zhang Village was in its final stages, and that they had found nothing on Zhang Guiquan, the murderous deputy village chief. After that, word filtered out that "some of the representatives [those doing the auditing] themselves may well end up behind bars." What's more, Zhang Guiquan's son number four threatened, "It's too early to call a truce, there must be some more bloodletting!" It seemed as if an evil wind was blowing stealthily through the village, carrying the smell of blood, choking the inhabitants.

Zhang Jiayu was a Party member who was an upright man and had been actively involved in protesting the excessive taxes all along. As a member of the audit group, he was the one who dared to raise questions without mincing words. Deputy Village Chief Zhang Guiquan hated Zhang Jiayu to the very marrow. On the day of the killings, Zhang Guiquan and his sons, after killing four people, thirsted for more blood, and the first person they had in mind was Zhang Jiayu. Son number six had shouted, "C'mon, let's deal with Zhang Jiayu! Don't leave anyone in his family alive!" Luckily for Zhang Jiayu, he was not home; he had gone off to report the atrocities being committed, and thus escaped being killed. To this day, Zhang Jiayu has no peace and feels himself to be in danger on a daily basis, possibly being followed. Sometimes he sees suspicious-looking characters lurking outside his house.

As to the murderous village tyrant Zhang Guiquan, his family was still a power to be reckoned with in the village. Besides, Zhang Leyi, number seven son, was still on the loose, and who knew when he might show up again. The villagers, especially the victims' families, had no sense of security. The old mother of the murdered brothers was inconsolable. In one afternoon she had lost two sons, and her grandson Pine had been wounded. A happy family was destroyed. And the nightmare was not over. The old mother said, showing fear and trepidation, "No one dares go out at night. Even in daytime, no one dares go far. Too scared to tend the peanuts, even in broad daylight."

The Press Arrive at Last

What next transpired was beyond imagination.

As mentioned, the township had dispatched cadres to call a general meeting at Zhang Village to warn the victims' family members not to "blab." The county TV station and the provincial newspapers referred to the killings as "manslaughter," the result of "fighting among ignorant peasants." Of course these pronouncements did not carry legal weight. Even the inhabitants of Zhang Village, who were not well versed in legal issues, knew that the last word on the matter would be had by the People's Procurator and the People's Court. Yet, strangely, when the case started to unravel, the legal machinery failed. The local court degenerated into a representative of local special interests. It was at this point that the inhabitants of Zhang Village were truly overcome with fear and despair.

When the Bengbu Intermediate Court began to try the case, they had no intention of informing the victims' families. When the families did finally hear about it, their legal representatives did not even have time to hire a lawyer.

Zhang Jiayu, the Party member who was village representative, swore by his twenty-five years' Party membership that the court investigators had never even set foot in the village, let alone interviewed witnesses regarding the facts of the case. No one had a clue as to what charges the prosecution had filed. The victims' families and witnesses only knew through hearsay that the trial was about to take place and rushed to the court, but were allowed in only as spectators. Worse, the accused, Zhang Guiquan and his sons, sat in the courtroom visibly at ease, whispering to each other. The victims' families were distraught.

Again, during the sentencing phase, the victims' families were not formally notified. When they rushed over after hearing of the news, they learned that the main culprits and directors of the killing, Zhang Guiquan and son number one, Zhang Jiazhi, who had killed Zhang Guiyue, had been given the death sentence. Son number six, Zhang Chaowei, and son number five, Zhang Yuliang, who had killed the village representatives Zhang Guiyu and Zhang Hongchuan, were both given life sentences. Justice had not been done; obviously, the sentences were meant to make one of the sons pay for the crimes of all the others.

The victims' families demanded to see a copy of the sentencing document, but the courts would not release it to them. The victims' families delegated their lawyers to ask for a copy of the sentence, but the court stood by its decision and stoutly refused, spouting a lot of legalese.

Zhang Jiayu, a graduate of the county high school, had the most schooling among the peasants of Zhang Village. He looked in the official copy of the civil code and discovered that paragraph 128 stipulated in black and white that "in the event that the victim or the legal representative of the victim is not satisfied with the sentence of the local court, they have the right, within five days of being informed of the sentence, to appeal to the People's Procurator to dispute the sentence." Thus, it was clear that according to state law, the Bengbu Intermediate Court had no right to refuse to show a copy of the sentence to the victims and their legal representatives. They had denied the victims and their representatives their legal right, and this could not be explained away as an oversight.

The victims' families now went to the High Court of Anhui Province.

The Anhui court finally directed that they be given a copy— not of the sentence handed down by the Bengbu Intermediate Court but of the prosecution charges, filed as Bengbu civil case 21. When the victims' families laid eyes on the charges, they had the shock of their lives. There was no mention at all that Zhang Guiyu and his fellow victims had been village represen- tatives charged with auditing the village books, no mention that they were trying to discharge their civic duties as entrusted to them by the eighty-seven households of Zhang Village, and no mention that Zhang Guiquan, the accused, had deliberately taken deadly revenge on the victims for checking on the village finances, including his own financial irregularities. The case summary was silent on the true background of the tragedy, which was the fact that the villagers were overburdened beyond endurance and demanded to check the village finances, where- upon the cadres had murdered in order to avoid the audit and cover their tracks. There was no mention that the instigator of the so-called fight was Zhang Jie, son of the village accountant, and that Zhang Guiquan's son number seven had exacerbated the situation by swearing at Zhang Guiyu for taking part in the auditing. In other words, the core events of the tragedy were covered up. At the same time, the charges did make mention of the words of protest made by Wei Surong, the wife of the first victim, Zhang Guiyu, when the Zhang father and sons rudely invaded her home. But Wei's remark was framed as the source of the violence and the tragedy, as the spark that set off a bout of mutual recriminations. Furthermore, the formal charges did not explain the presence of the two sons of Zhang Guiquan in Wei Surong's house. Since they had nothing to do with the auditing, what were they doing in the company of their father, and what account, if any, did they have to settle with the victim Zhang Guiyu? The charges were silent on the actual subject matter of the so-called mutual "recriminations"—namely, the need to audit the village finances.

According to the prosecution's document, Zhang Guiyu and his wife Wei Surong were the first to take up weapons in the confrontation, and Zhang Guiyu and the other victim, Zhang Hongchuan, were the first to attack. As for Zhang Guiquan's son number one, who had killed without batting an eyelash, he was described as having picked up his knife only when he saw Zhang Guiyu and Zhang Hongchuan "on the point of" attacking his own father; such imprecise language was used throughout the case report to muddy the waters and create confusion as to what really had happened. The case file notes that later on, when this same son number one saw Zhang Guiyu straddling the back of his brother son number six, only then did he deal that last blow and finish him off. And this son number six, supposedly held down by Zhang Guiyu, was reported as only being able to join the fight after he was able to get to his feet, stress being laid on the expression "get to his feet."

In a word, according to the charges in the Bengbu Intermediate Court case file number 21, it was the village representatives or their families who started the hostilities, who first picked up weapons, and who first attacked. The report implied that these village representatives who had been killed had been asking for it.

The explanation of how Zhang Guiyu's son, Pine, had been wounded was even more ludicrous. According to the information quoted in the file, Zhang Guiquan's son number five had snatched a club from the hands of Zhang Guiyu (who by then had fallen heavily to the ground) and dealt a blow to the latter's son, Pine. The fact was, this one strike had left a wound two and a half inches long and almost three inches deep in Pine's shoulder, and put Pine in the hospital for a whole month. The magazine *Democracy and Law* later printed a photograph of Pine's wound, belying the wording of the case file. The Bengbu Intermediate Court prosecuted the murder as a case of "inflicting bodily harm, which resulted in death." This totally changed the nature of this case, which is in essence a case of violent attempted murder. To inflict bodily harm refers to harming someone's health and well-being, whereas trying to deprive someone of life, as in this case, is plain attempted murder. In fact, the forensic evidence is sufficient to show that the perpetrators aimed for the heart and other vital organs and were out to kill. Zhang Hongchuan died from "a single knife wound in the chest which ruptured the main artery of the heart, leading to massive hemorrhage. Zhang Guimao died of a single knife wound in the left side of the back, which punctured his left lung, leading to massive hemorrhage. Zhang Guiyu died of a single knife wound in the chest, which punctured his heart and lung, leading to massive hemorrhage; his brother Zhang Guiyue died of a single knife wound in the left side of his chest, which punctured the left lung, leading to massive hemorrhage. Zhang

Guiyu's son, Pine, was spared his life because he turned his head, and the meat cleaver aimed at his head landed on his shoulder.

If killing four people within a matter of minutes is considered "inflicting bodily harm," what does it take to constitute "murder"?

Everyone who heard Zhang Guiquan bellow, "Kill! Kill! Twelve bastards trying to check my books, kill them all!" had been shocked at his animal-like rage, yet the case file would not, or dared not, include these words in the record.

Although the Bengbu Intermediate Court did not prosecute Zhang Guiquan for murder, ironically, he did not appreciate the favor. When the sentence was read out in court, he actually exploded in anger, and vowed that his sons would stick a knife into the judge when they were released! An instigator and organizer of multiple killings actually dared to bare his teeth in a court of law; one wonders what the prosecutor and his deputy, who had signed their names to the sentence, thought of this performance.

Two thousand years ago, in the era of the Han Dynasty (206 B.C.–A.D. 220), Huan Kuan wrote in his treatise *On Salt and Iron* that a society does not suffer for want of laws, but from want of orders to implement laws. It is fatal, he wrote, to pass laws and not implement them.

We usually refer to the supervisory power of the law as the "fourth power," after the Party, the government, and the army; the law is an important force to ensure social justice and righteousness. But even to this day, in many places, what determines the victory or failure of a lawsuit is not the rights and wrongs of the case itself, but rather, the petitioners' ability to get access to the justice system. The inviolable law and its rightful authority cannot be upheld, and the independence of the legal process becomes only words written on paper, if the law cannot be appealed to. In fact there is another, more powerful force operating, creating a distance between our life as it is lived and the letter of the law. To prevent the peasants of Zhang Village from going to Beijing to appeal cases and present petitions to the courts, the Guzhen County railway station employees actually interrogated the peasants closely before they were allowed to buy a ticket. Two peasants from the Guzhen area who wanted to visit with relatives in Beijing and seek medical advice there had to do a lot of explaining; only after proving without a doubt that they were not from Tangnan Township and were not going to make complaints at the capital were they finally allowed to get on the train.

This kind of control was futile, of course. How could all activities in the vastness of China be controlled by a few prohibitions? Eventually, news of the tragedy at Zhang Village did get out, and eventually it attracted the attention of the media.

The first media people who came to do on-the-spot investigations were reporters from the Anhui branch of the Xinhua News Agency. After their investigation, Li Renhu and Ge Renjiang wrote "Get-Rich-Quick Tricks by Cadres of Zhang Village: One Payment, Two Records," an article on the fraud perpetrated by the village cadres to cover the excessive tax burdens imposed on the peasants. Although the article did not mention the murders committed in the village, the facts presented provided the background for understanding what happened, and was reprinted in the national papers. It began with the reporters' arrival in Zhang Village for interviews and described how the villagers showed them the trick practiced by the local cadres of recording payments in two different versions, one figure that was minimized for the benefit of inspectors from their superiors, and another, higher figure, the true figure, which was what the peasants were forced to pay.

For example, Zhang Jiayu took out the records of his payments for the years 1996 and 1997 in dual versions—on official cards and on plain paper. For the year 1996, the official card recorded that the previous year, Zhang Jiayu's family of five with two working adults under contract for 12.65 *mu* (about 19 acres) of arable land had paid 6.1 percent of their income in taxes, but they had actually paid 19.8 percent of their income in taxes and other payments, 13.7 percentage points more than the official record. For the year 1997, the official percentage of his income paid in taxes was 7 percent, but the real percentage was 22.7, making a gap of 15.7 percentage points between the true and the false record of payments.

According to the article, Zhang Village and its affiliated areas comprised 142 households, with a total population of 750. It was an exclusively agricultural area situated in the lowlands neighboring the Huai River. It was prone to floods and the people were poor. The reporter went through many households without seeing a decent piece of furniture or furnishing; many households couldn't even afford a black and white television set. But most cadres owned refrigerators and color televisions, and some of them even lived in multistory mansions. The villagers all complained that the cadres cheated their superiors and oppressed the people, gave themselves perks and privileges and did not keep proper records of the village finances. The "one payment, two records" scam was just one item in their bag of dirty tricks.

Following the publication of the Li Renhu–Ge Renjiang report, a journalist from the influential *Trade and Industry Daily Guide* published an article titled "Zhang Guiquan Must Answer to the Law for the Deaths of Four People" that did not mince words about the murder. This article went to the heart of the problem by stating in its headlines: "Still serving a sentence, this man became a village cadre; he has something to hide and opposes auditing; four members of auditing group killed in broad daylight."

Following the article in *Trade and Industry Daily Guide*, the paper *Wenhui Trade and Industry* published on its front page a piece titled "A Truthful Report on a Case of Aggravated Murder in Guzhen County." These articles finally set the true facts of the killings in Zhang Village before the public, defeating all the cover-up attempts of the Guzhen County and Bengbu municipal Party authorities.

About four months after the tragedy, on a hot early-summer afternoon, four reporters from China Central Television trudged their dusty way to Zhang Village carrying their heavy equipment on their shoulders. They had seen the Xinhua News Agency story on "one payment, two records," which had been wired nationwide, and on June 15, 1998, they decided to come and see for themselves. Once in the village they started talking to people casually and taking pictures at random.

They walked into the house of Huang Zhiwei and asked him, "How much is your annual burden of taxes?" Huang was obviously ill at ease, but after a long hesitation, he showed them his official report card of payments and the real payments scrawled on pieces of plain paper. "Yes, it is a heavy burden," he said.

The reporters interviewed the upstanding village representative, Zhang Jiayu, whom they found working in the fields. Zhang Jiayu gave the reporters more information about the cadres' practice of issuing two records for the same payments. He went on to tell them the whole story of how the representatives decided to check the village books for evidence of Zhang Guiquan's embezzlement of public funds, and how Zhang came out in full force with his sons and killed four people. The reporters asked Zhang Jiayu to lead the way, and they went to see the orphans of the murdered Zhang Guimao and Zhang Hongchuan and offered their condolences.

Finally the reporters asked Zhang Jiayu to take them to the house of the village Party boss, Zhang Dianfeng, hoping to interview him. It turned out that the Party head was not at home, so the reporters decided to interview his wife, Chen Yunxia. To their surprise, Chen was very hostile. First she shut the door in the reporters' faces. Then she came out of the house, locked the door behind her, shouldered a hoe, and went her way to the fields. The reporters did not take it personally. Cameras in hand, they seized this rare chance to follow her, shooting all the way, until she was out of sight.

The reporters were just about to leave when they saw some-one walking toward the house, steering a bike with one hand. It was obviously Zhang Dianfeng. From a distance the reporters followed the man's movements. A bunch of villagers were shouting something at him, and finally the man caught sight of the camera aimed at him. Probably sensing that something was wrong, he turned to flee; then changing his mind, he turned around and walked back toward the reporters.

The reporters went up to him and asked, "Are you the Party head for the village?"

"Yes."

"May we talk to you?"

Zhang Dianfeng had by now recovered his composure. "Of course, let's talk in my house," he answered readily. But on arrival he was met by the big lock hanging on the door, the key taken away by his wife. Zhang was visibly embarrassed.

The reporters decided to talk to him then and there. "Are the financial records of your village open to the public?"

Zhang Dianfeng replied readily, "Of course the records are open. Daily recordings, monthly summing ups. The records are posted for public review every fifth of the month."

"Posted? Where?" the reporters asked.

"Posted in each of the three village localities."

"Where exactly are they posted in the three localities? Have you seen them?'

Zhang Dianfeng hesitated a second before saying, "I don't see them myself, but I give out assignments to have them posted."

Amused, the reporters bombarded him with more questions as the villagers, who had by now crowded around them, laughed out loud at Zhang Dianfeng's lies. Someone shouted, "The Party boss is talking through his hat!" amid more laughter.

Zhang Dianfeng wiped the smile from his face, and glowered at the group in front of him.

Just then, the village representative, Zhang Jiayu, emerged from the crowd, walked right up to the camera, and said in a loud voice, "The village records have never ever been made public in Zhang Village!"

Zhang Dianfeng turned to the speaker and growled, "Zhang Jiayu! Do you count yourself a Communist Party member? The records are posted and you never saw them? Are you doing your duty as a Party member?"

Obviously, according to Zhang Dianfeng, every Party member who was worth his salt must be in lockstep with him or be disqualified as a Party member.

The whole scene was caught on camera.

That same night, or, more precisely, at 2 A.M. the next morning, the Party leader of Tangnan Township phoned Zhang Dianfeng, asking about the details of the reporters' visit. Whom had they talked to? What about? Had anybody said anything about the auditing and the village representatives who had been killed? And so on and so forth. These local leaders acted as if they were under siege by a deadly enemy.

Two days after the reporters' visit, the village chief, Zhang

Fengchi, went on the attack. This illiterate boor raved and ranted in the village broadcast,* "Some individual Communist Party members snuck a few rotten reporters into our village, telling them that everything here is a patchwork of lies. They also dragged over some reporters from the *Core Issues* TV program with their blather. Who cares for their core issues? As I see it, some people are out to make trouble. Okay, go on with your underhanded dealings. Wait till I catch you!"

The village chief was shouting at the top of his voice and had cranked the amplifier's volume up to the highest level so that the villagers felt as if their ears were being blasted by an explosion. Rudely awakened in the early hours of the morning, they couldn't help wondering, what kind of creatures, after all, were running Zhang Village?

On the evening of June 20, the TV series *The Fabric of Our Society* beamed a report on how the cadres of Zhang Village fleeced the peasants, putting the story in the national headlines.

Soon, the *Southern Weekender* used the whole of its front page to expose the bloody murders in Zhang Village, publishing a long report by Zhu Qing titled "Father and Four Sons Tyrannizing a Village Will Stop at Nothing; Villagers Intent on Auditing the Books Are Stopped by Murder." The front page also featured a series of cartoons by the cartoonist Fang Tang. He portrayed village leaders feasting and drinking at public expense, one picture showing their desks laden with wine bottles, and another showing them with cigarettes stuck between their lips as they stepped over the bodies of peasants bent prostrate before them. The article matching the cartoon was written by Dang Guoyin, a fellow of the Chinese Academy of Social Sciences, in Beijing. Guoyin's indignation fairly burst off the

*In some areas it was standard practice for each village household to be fitted with a speaker that could not be turned off.

page: "We have a government that has signed the international convention regarding human rights, and after all we are in a civilized age, how could we tolerate such rampant evil among us." He pointed out, "It is of course necessary to discipline the cadres who violate the policies and laws of the country, and such discipline will probably bear results to a certain extent, but that is only scratching the surface of the problem. A thorough solution is to allow the peasants to be well-to-do, to allow them to organize themselves, and to confer legal status on their organization so that the peasants will be empowered to resist the political machine in the countryside."

Around this time, three reporters from the magazine *Democracy and Law* also went down to Zhang Village, and published their on-the-site report in the seventeenth issue of their journal. The title was blunt—"Villagers' Representatives Trying to Audit the Village Books Were Brutally Murdered"— and the report was riveting in its graphic description and thunderous in its denunciation. One very curious fact first revealed in this report was that one of the murder weapons, the bloody knife that had been wielded by Zhang Guiquan's son number six, was still lying in a drawer in the village clinic and had been totally overlooked all this while. The reporters took a photo of this piece of evidence and published it along with their report.

With the media's attention now focused on the crime and numerous articles appearing in the national press, the case of peasants being killed because they wanted to audit the village books could not be covered up any longer. Only then did things take a turn for the better.

Tangnan Township officials took steps to provide for the two orphans of the dead Zhang Hongchuan.

At the Dragon Boat Festival, which fell on the fifth day of the fifth month by the lunar calendar, the county government gave one hundred yuan in consolation money to each of the afflicted families.

Moreover, during the harvest following the Dragon Boat Festival, several officials from the Guzhen County administration came down to the village and helped the afflicted families take in the harvest, working through a long morning without complaining of tiredness, nor touching a drop of water nor a grain of the families' rice. This went some way toward conveying to the families the warmth of the Party's and government's concern for them.

On August 8, 1998, the High Court of Anhui Province issued the final sentence on the case of Zhang Guiquan and his sons. The sentence and the list of charges differed little from that of the Bengbu Intermediate Court, and the peasants of Zhang Village could not help being disappointed at the legal system.

But from one important point the villagers drew some comfort: in the final paragraph of the indictment it was pointed out that Zhang Guiquan and his sons had no grounds for claiming self-defense, that the offense of Zhang Guiquan and his eldest son, Zhang Jiazhi, sixth son, Zhang Chaowei, and fifth son, Zhang Yuliang, was not merely intent to "inflict bodily harm" but that they had committed acts of violence with intent to kill, and that their claim of lack of intent to kill was without merit and could not be considered. That was some consolation to the villagers of Zhang Village, which had been devastated by the crime.

3

THE LONG AND THE SHORT OF THE "ANTITAX UPRISING"

Where the Emperor Bade Farewell to his Concubine

Gaixia, the scene of a famous battle more than two thousand years ago, in 202 B.C., lies within today's Lingbi County, Anhui Province. This is where the Han king Liu Bei and the Shu king Xiang Yu fought to the death for supremacy over control of what would later be known as the Middle Kingdom.* Xiang Yu's army of a hundred thousand men was surrounded in the town of Gaixia. King Liu, in coordination with his aide Han Xin, amassed an army four hundred thousand strong and encircled Xiang Yu's army so tightly that not a drop of water could seep in, let alone reinforcements. Under siege and starving, Xiang Yu's hundred thousand troops lost the will to fight when echoes of their native Shu songs wafted over the town walls, deluding them into thinking that these were the sounds of their fellow Shu men who had been taken into captivity. In fact, it was a trick played by the Han king. This was the setting for the tragedy of Xiang Yu's concubine Yu, who snatched her lord's sword and killed herself so as not to encumber her lord in his last desperate battle to break the siege and save his men. Her

*The Middle Kingdom (Zhongguo) is an ancient name for China that is still used in modern China.

act of supreme loyalty is remembered down the ages in history, art, and legend, the best-known example being the classic Beijing opera *The King Bids Farewell to His Concubine*.

Since that momentous historical event, whose outcome was the founding of the Han Dynasty, the years have rolled by, and this patch of poor barren land has lain dormant and forgotten, as if time had stopped. But at noon on a sunny day, October 5, 1997, the silence was broken by the rumbling wheels of modern transportation. A convoy of police cars, sedans, trucks, and even fire engines started out from Lingbi County, enhanced by the forbidding presence of a selection of local Party and government officials—in an outrageous display of sartorial preferences. Police sirens cleared the way as the convoy rumbled onward, raising clouds of dust, while an array of weapons gleamed in the sunlight. Such a show of power, pomp, and circumstance was totally unprecedented in the history of Lingbi County.

People living nearby hastily made way for this armed cavalcade, while frightened eyes peering from behind cottage windows counted the number of vehicles—thirty-two altogether, carrying over two hundred personnel.

From Fengmiao Township the armed convoy made a turn for the southeast and, about ten kilometers later, arrived at Gao Village. The armed police immediately hopped down and sealed all the exits from the village. The Fengmiao Township Party boss, Hou Chaojie, sent for the Gao Village Party boss, Chen Yiwen, and the village chief, Gao Xuewen. With the two Party bosses leading the way, a group of fully armed public security officers descended on the western section of the village like a wolf on the fold. The battle ended as swiftly as it began, and a resounding victory was declared less than fifteen minutes later.

It was the noon break, and the inhabitants of Gao Village were totally unprepared for any kind of conflict. The women were bustling over the cooking while the men had just returned from the fields. Many of them had tossed off their jackets and shoes. They were stunned when armed security men materialized in front of them, and no one thought of reaching for an object to use in self-defense.

The fully armed detachment of officers and their men, suddenly faced with a motley crowd of totally defenseless, barefoot peasants, were themselves taken by surprise—they were unprepared for this somewhat anticlimactic victory. Nevertheless, the spoils of victory were impressive: except for the handful of people who were still planting seedlings in the rice paddies, or were at the market, or were migrant workers employed in the city, this military action made a clean sweep of all the suspects; not a single one eluded the lawmen's net.

The population of the western side of Gao village numbered barely a hundred heads; now, fifty-one had been arrested in one fell swoop—or fifty-two if you counted a three-year old toddler who was arrested along with his mother. This so-called "Gao Village incident" sent shock waves through millions of inhabitants of the provinces of Anhui and neighboring Jiangsu.

When the "Gao Village incident" occurred, two magazines in Hong Kong were already publishing reports of widespread rural unrest, disturbances, riots, and even armed uprising on the mainland under such titles as "Peasants' Uprising Spreads Through Several Provinces" and "Half a Million Peasants in Four Provinces Stand Up for Their Rights." These particular reports were unfounded, but the problems they touched on were undeniable. Our own investigation showed that the General Office of the Party Central Committee and of the State Council had issued joint directives, warning: "Many of our local Party and government leaders do not know how to handle the new situation and new problems cropping up in the rural areas today. On the contrary, they resort to security forces, armed police and militia, thus aggravating the situation." Although the "Gao Village incident" was labeled a violent "antitax uprising" by the local authorities, in truth there was no resistance at all. When villagers heard the screaming sirens and saw the police convoy arrive, they thought that the security forces were doing their job and were coming to arrest Village Chief Gao Xuewen!

The so-called "Gao village incident" was merely the last episode in a story fabricated by Gao Xuewen, the village chief. It is a long story.

To begin at the beginning, Gao Xuewen was universally hated in Gao Village. Ever since worming his way to the position of village chief, the man had been walking on clouds with his nose in the air, seeming to have even forgotten the surname of his own ancestors. No matter how many documents and directives were passed down from the Party Central Committee on relieving the peasants' burden, the amount of taxes and dues in Gao Village still depended on Gao Xuewen's word. You had to pay exactly what he ordered, and not a cent less. Opposing Gao was tantamount to opposing the people's government, even the Party. If you were so unfortunate as to get into his bad books, he had no compunction against cursing and striking you. Not enough to be beaten and abused, the injured party was obliged to apologize before the matter was allowed to end.

The police action of October 5, 1997, did not come out of the blue but was, rather, the culmination of a series of events that was triggered by a minor affair, when Gao Xuewen once again had a chance to show his power. One of the respected village elders, seventy-year-old Granny Gao, had ventured to challenge the double tax for the site of her house. Gao Xuewen, contrary to the cultured flavor of his name (a combination of the words "study" and "literary"), reacted like a bully, ransacking the house and smashing pots and pans and attacking the inhabitants. This was on October 4. As usual, it was the guilty party who rushed to make accusations. Gao Xuewen not only escaped reprimand but by his maneuvers managed on the very next day to return in triumph with security officers and armed police in tow, who started arresting people right and left, leaving the whole village stunned.

The first to be arrested during the afternoon of October 5 was Granny Gao. Not satisfied with arresting her, the police arrested her entire immediate family. Still not satisfied, they went on to arrest her elder and younger brothers, who were visiting, as well as her nephew and also her brother-in-law on her husband's side. In short, the police grabbed everybody present in the house, whether from her or her husband's side of the family, ten people altogether from a family gathering of eleven. The only one left behind was a ninety-year-old grandmother-in-law, a bedridden invalid. Granny Gao was being dragged to the police car when it was noticed that her cheeks still bore the marks of Gao Xuewen's blows from the day before. It would not do to let her show her face with all those telling marks, so she was pushed out of the car at the last moment.

Meanwhile, there had been an interesting little interlude during the raid.

The day before, some neighbors had not been able to bear to sit by with their hands folded while the poor, defenseless old woman was knocked about by the brute of a village chief. So they went to the neighboring county, Gaoji, and hired a photographer to record the evidence of what had been done to Granny Gao. There was a national drive to disseminate legal information among the peasants, which was why they even had such an idea. The photographer, a woman, arrived on October 5 and had finished taking pictures of Granny Gao's battered face and was just about to photograph the state of the ransacked room when Gao Xuewen arrived with his gang. At the sight of the photographer collecting the evidence, a furious Gao Xuewen not only arrested Granny Gao but seized the photographer as well.

The woman photographer had seen something of the world. Totally unimpressed by Gao and the gang, she said contemptuously, "Watch your step. I am not from your county!" One member of the invading group, the cashier of the township financial office, was provoked beyond endurance by the photographer's attitude. He pointed a finger at the woman and swore, "Even if you were the wife of Jiang Zemin or Li Peng, you will get a taste of my power!"*

Everyone present was stunned.

"Take her away!" the cashier commanded in a thunderous voice.

The woman barely deigned to give the impertinent cashier a look. Not at all intimidated, she retorted in a level voice, "Truthfully speaking, I can't pretend to have such lofty connections, but I'll tell you what—the deputy head of your county security bureau is a relative of mine. You are welcome to check." That left the crowd even more stunned.

The security people took notice. Reluctant to take her at her word, it was also risky to totally shrug her off. Thus, when the photographer was taken away with the rest, the armed police as

---

*Jiang Zemin (born August 17, 1926) served as general secretary of the Communist Party of China from 1989 to 2002; as president of the People's Republic from 1993 to 2003; and as chairman of the Central Military Commission from 1989 to 2004.

Li Peng (born in 1928) was the chairman of the Standing Committee of the National People's Congress of the People's Republic of China (PRC) from 1998 to 2003 and was second-ranking in the Chinese Communist Party, behind Jiang Zemin. He served as premier of the State Council between 1987 and 1998. Concerned about maintaining social and political stability, Li promoted a cautious approach toward Chinese economic reform.

well as the security people restrained themselves—even acted conciliatory.

Another minor episode during the mass arrest related to the white-bearded Gao Zongpeng, a man who had long seen through the tricks of the village cadres, and would leap to the defense of the weak and defenseless at the drop of a hat. The village leadership considered Gao Zongpeng a typical trouble-maker. When Gao Zongpeng saw the crowd from the county and the township storming Gao Village, arresting people right and left, quite predictably he stuck his neck out and scolded the village cadres: "You sons of turtles, don't go too far! Do you want to provoke a peasant uprising?" Gao Zongpeng was already on the village chief's black list, so sticking his head out just made matters easier. The county and township gang arrested him and took away his two sons and a daughter-in-law into the bargain.

That was how fifty-two people were arrested: seventy-year-olds and toddlers, war veterans and long-time Party members, including many women old and young.

One could see at a glance that the arrested group included the "undesirables" of Gao Village: those who had gone to higher authorities to complain about excessive taxes, those who had voiced suspicions about the village financial records, and others who had differences of one kind or another with the village authorities. Under the guise of dealing with Granny Gao, the village leadership tried to get rid of everyone they considered a thorn in their side.

Since the raid was a joint action hastily arranged by forces from different departments, none of whom were familiar with the villagers, the raiders' show of force landed them with a mot-ley crowd on their hands. Caught in the net with Granny Gao and the local troublemakers were outsiders who had come to visit relatives or to help with the harvest, and there were even some entrepreneurs who had come on business. And it was complete mayhem, because these law enforcement officers came from different departments, such as security and militia, and they took the individuals they had arrested back to their own headquarters, so the show of force ended up by separating families. When the police cars and other vehicles started off with their prizes, the air was rent by screams and wailing as parents looked for children, and brother called to sister. The old and the sick left behind later recalled the scene with horror. It reminded them of the invading Japanese army, they commented bitterly, except that these villains did not speak Japanese.

All the arrested were questioned the same night, the only exception being the woman photographer from the neighboring county. A short investigation revealed that her family indeed had some tenuous relationship with one of the many deputy heads of the county security office, and she was quietly released. As for the others, they were all made to pay "fines" to be released. In the end many villagers had to borrow money at high interest to buy their freedom and found themselves weighed down by as much as ten thousand yuan in debt. Some were totally ruined; others became migrant workers in cities to making a living.

The nephew of Granny Gao, a hot-blooded young man, could not control his temper at the blackmail. As a result, he got kicked so hard in the shins that he was lamed for a month, and was forced to pay the "fine" down to the last penny. When he was finally released from detention, he was steeped in bitterness, all his youthful illusions swept away.

One Day and One Night in Gao Village

To get back into the chain of events that culminated in the raid requires starting at the beginning with more detail. In 1990, Granny Gao's house was rebuilt on the foundation of an earlier house and had never encroached on arable land. During decollectivization, the land had already been counted toward her allotment of arable land, and she was taxed annually like everybody else. In addition, there was a one-time "house-site tax" to be paid, which she had paid in 1996. But on October 4, 1997, one day before the raid, she had been asked again to pay the 110 yuan house-site tax. Village Chief Gao Xuewen had once again appeared at her door and demanded payment of the house-site tax. Granny asked in surprise, "But haven't I paid it already?" The village chief, not accustomed to being questioned, ordered her, "Do as you are told! Pay up and pay in full. I have no time for your nonsense!"

Granny wanted to get the matter cleared up once and for all. "Last year," she reminded him, "I paid one hundred ten yuan, and you said that I was in the clear. Why you are here again?"

Village Chief Gao, losing patience, raised his voice. "Paid? To whom?"

Granny had long been upset by the village cadres' practice of making a scrawl on a scrap of paper instead of giving a proper receipt for payments. So she retorted, "I paid it to the star of the night. You should know that!"

Village Chief Gao did not expect to be rebuffed by an old granny. He took a step back and looked the old woman up and down as if not quite believing his eyes. Then he stepped up to the frail old lady and issued an ultimatum: "Pay up, or accept the consequences."

Trembling with anger, Granny shouted back at him, "No way!"

Village Chief Gao, shocked at the force of the old woman's defiance, raised his voice even higher. "I'll see to it that you are charged with an antitax crime!"

The loud altercation attracted a number of villagers, who took Granny's side, saying that the village chief had no right to demand another payment of the one-time house-site tax.

Village Chief Gao was losing face in front of people whom he considered his inferiors. He turned fiercely on Granny again and said, "You paid? Where's the proof?"

Granny Gao, provoked beyond endurance, went up to the bully, pointed her finger at him, and demanded, "Dare you swear—"

Before she had finished the sentence, Gao Xuewen swung his arm and gave the old lady a resounding whack on her cheek. She tottered, almost losing balance, and a big purple bruise immediately started to appear and her cheek started to swell.

The shocked villagers gathered around and began berating Gao for hitting an elder.

The pig-headed Gao did not give an inch. "So what if I hit her? I'm going to raid her house, just you watch!" And then and there he stomped into Granny's house like a wild beast, smashing pots and pans and everything in sight.

Having vented his rage, the village chief walked away.

Poor Granny fainted.

Thus ended the first in the chain of events that preceded the Gao Village incident.

Seeing the village chief apparently beating a retreat, the villagers agreed that this time he had gone too far. They were not surprised to see Zheng Jianmin, the deputy chief of the Fengmiao Township security station, show up at around one o'clock in the early afternoon, soon after Village Chief Gao's departure. They were all gleefully looking forward to seeing how the village chief would be dealt with by township security after attacking an old lady and wrecking her home.

But instead of hauling over the village chief, as the villagers expected, Deputy Security Chief Zheng Jianmin headed straight for Granny Gao's place, followed by his men in a police car. Without any explanation, he went in and tried to arrest Granny and her son. The villagers could not believe their eyes. They proceeded to tell Zheng what had really happened in the morning and advised him not to arrest innocent people. But the security chief wouldn't listen to them. He had already heard Village Chief Gao Xuewen's version of the story, and did not want to hear anything else.

"Who is arresting innocent people?" he asked angrily.

"You are!" the villagers retorted.

"Why don't you do some investigation?" one villager added.

In recent years, many villagers had been to the city as migrant workers and they had some inkling of how things are run in a more modern society; it was obvious to them that Zheng was violating regulations.

Zheng Jianmin looked at the villagers contemptuously; to him, they were born to toil on the land and were not worthy of his attention. Just then, a man who seemed to stand above the rest of the villagers walked out from the crowd. He was Gao Guanghua.

Gao Guanghua confronted Deputy Security Chief Zheng face to face: "Gao Xuewen served Granny with a duplicate demand for payment of a one-time house-site tax. So he was wrong in the first place. Then he hit her, which is an additional offense. On top of that he wrecked Granny's house, which constitutes a third legal offense. If you security officers actually believe his story, how can we common people ever trust you to protect us?"

Said right in front of the villagers, Gao Guanghua's words to the security officer caused the latter to lose face. In a harsh voice, he rapped out an order to his men: "Take him away!"

Gao Guanghua struggled against Zheng's men, shouting, "What right do you have to arrest me?" Zheng answered, "You are obstructing me in carrying out official duties." Zheng's men overpowered Gao Guanghua and threw him into the police car.

By now the villagers were thoroughly agitated; they surrounded Zheng and accused him of abusing his authority. Zheng, cornered, pulled out his gun. "What are you trying to do?" he asked hysterically. He pointed the weapon now at one villager, now at another.

At this point the white-haired old man called Gao Zongpeng, who had been watching the scene quietly from the sidelines, now came forward and confronted Zheng. "Remember, you are supposed to be the people's security force. And now without any investigation, without giving people a chance to say a word, you actually threaten us villagers with a gun. You are completely lawless!" The old man put his face up to Zheng's gun and taunted him, "Fire, if you have the guts. Aim here! We villagers may be worthless in your eyes, but we are not afraid to die!"

Zheng Jianmin was wavering, and the old man pressed on: "If this is called obstructing official business, then we are all obstructing your business. Go ahead and arrest us all! Can you kill us all?! Who's afraid of that gun of yours?!" By then the villagers also crowded around to face down Zheng and his gun, saying, "Fire! Go ahead and fire if you have the balls!"

Faced with the fury of the crowd, Zheng's hand began to waver, and finally he holstered the gun, but not before giving the white-haired old man a piercing look, as if to imprint his image and remember to settle the score later. During this set-to the other villagers had managed to rescue Gao Guanghua from the police car.

Stony-faced, Zheng jumped into the police vehicle without saying a word. Slamming the door shut, he sped off, leaving behind a trail of dust and smoke.

The crowd in front of Granny Gao's house dispersed, laughing at how the deputy chief of Fengmiao Township security had slunk away.

Thus ended the second episode in the chain of events that led up to the Gao Village incident.

* * *

Old Gao Zongpeng did not share the villagers' confidence that they had cowed the deputy security chief. He said to himself, "That gang will never give up so easily. How can they bear to be put down by us mere country bumpkins? They're bound to find an excuse to come back for revenge in a big way." He was right. This second episode ushered in a third

Just as the white-bearded old man feared, Deputy Security Chief Zheng Jianmin returned to the security station in Fengmiao Township and told the other officials what had happened. He made up his own version, adding many exaggerations and distortions. Security Chief Ma Li and Political Director Zhu of Fengmiao Township security were both men of some standing in the region. To them it was preposterous that the village bumpkins had actually gotten the better of one of their own. They promptly went to the administrative head and the Party boss of the township, adding their own embellishments to Zheng's story.

What followed was what the white-bearded old man had expected. Later in the afternoon of October 4, the same day of the events at Granny Gao's house, two vans showed up suddenly in the village, and a group of men emerged. Among them were Security Chief Ma Li; Political Director Zhu Xianmin; two deputy heads, of the township Party and administration, respectively; as well as a number of cadres from the township finance, trade, and tax offices.

This group of officials had come from Fengmiao Township, more than five miles away, and by now it was close to dusk. Villagers who saw them coming wondered what they were here for, and how they were going to conduct any business before their return to Fengmiao, since it would soon be dark.

The villagers were naïve enough to hope against hope that this batch of officials were going to deal with the outrages that had taken place that day: Village Chief Gao Xuewen's attack on Granny Gao in the morning and Deputy Security Chief Zheng's whipping out his gun and threatening villagers in the afternoon.

But this did not, after all, seem likely. The villagers followed the officials warily with their eyes and saw them looking around here and there, sometimes pointing with a finger at this and that, but never talking to anyone, never asking questions, much less doing anything to deal with the day's outrages. Then they made preparations to leave. The villagers were totally confused and asked one another, "What are they here for?"

A few villagers worked up the courage to approach the cadres and say that the village chief, Gao Xuewen, had attacked an old granny unprovoked that very morning and smashed up her house, and could the honorable gentlemen please look into the matter. But none of the township officials deigned to glance at these villagers, much less give them an answer as they got ready to step into their vans.

The villagers who had seen something of city life knew that the so-called leaders of the township, and even those from the county, were just small fry in the official hierarchy, what people would call "piddling sesame officials." They were thoroughly annoyed by the high and mighty airs these puffed-up petty township bureaucrats were putting on. Some of them muttered that this lot of "public servants" were downright bloodsuckers, not lifting a finger on behalf of the people who were feeding them. Others went a step further. They walked to the vans and said, "We can't stop you from going and we can't stop you from staying, but unless you deal with the problem of Gao Xuewen attacking people and smashing homes, the vans must stay."

One of the cadres demanded angrily, "What do you mean?"

One villager replied, "If you leave without a trace, where are we going to look for you to get justice in this case?" To everybody's surprise, one of the township leaders lost his temper. Raising his right hand as if signaling a final charge in a life-and-death struggle, he said in the tone of a tragic hero, "No one leave!" The villagers were not at all impressed. They thought to themselves: How easily provoked these people are. They travel to and fro in cars, spend their days sitting at headquarters looking at reports, and cannot cope with a whiff of real life.

None of the other cadres raised any objection to the command to stay, though no one had a clue as to why they were staying, and how and where they were going to spend the night. They walked in the direction of the house of Mrs. Gao Xuehua, the head of the village women's committee; her house was just a few steps away from where their vans were parked.

As if it were the most natural thing in the world, Mrs. Gao, seeing the group approach, put out tables and chairs, made tea, and laid cards on the table. While some of the men sat down and played cards, Mrs. Gao busied herself in the kitchen. Very soon it was like a party, with the men sipping tea, cracking melon seeds, and slapping cards on the table. Others dozed, or were just bored. Mrs. Gao soon produced a batch of crispy pancakes to go with fresh bean sprout soup. Someone managed to produce a carton of instant noodles, and the makeshift supper was complete.

It was common knowledge that eating and drinking were part of the daily official business of these public servants. Eating and drinking had become a branch of profound study at which these people excelled. So it was understandable that they found Mrs. Gao's pancakes and bean sprout soup to be not quite up to their standard, and very soon the floor was littered with half-eaten pancakes and leftover soup and noodles. During the greater part of the evening, many villagers lingered outside Mrs. Gao's house, watching the show and remarking on the shameful waste of food. Although they were at the bottom of the social heap, they were free to wag their tongues, and that night the villagers had a good time lashing out at these bloodsuckers. But no one could figure out why these public servants had decided to spend the night there, instead of in the comfort of their own homes.

Only white-bearded old Gao Zongpeng was uneasy. Tossing and turning in his bed, he could not make sense of the situation, but he knew that something fishy was going on. True, the villagers had urged these cadres to stay, but it was still very strange that the officials had stayed overnight in the village. It occurred to Gao Zongpeng that it was quite possible that these cadres might now claim that they had been kidnapped by the villagers.

The next day, October 5, 1997, dawned with the sun blazing in all its glory, sending its golden rays over the rooftops of the houses in Gao Village. No one except for Gao Zongpeng imagined what a day of disaster it would be for the villagers, a disaster that would cast a long shadow.

No one knew what the cadres were doing that night at Mrs. Gao's. The next morning, Zhu Xianmin, the political director of Fengmiao Township security, left the house early. The vans were parked nearby, but Zhu chose to return to the township by tractor; he was driven by the son of Village Chief Gao.

None of the villagers was aware that Zhu Xianmin had secretly left the village, and none could have conceived of the extent of the conspiracy. Who would have imagined that Zhu would rush back to Fengmiao to make a false report to the township Party boss, Hou Chaojie, and that Hou would go a step higher, to the Lingbi County Party Committee, and that the Lingbi Party bosses in turn would go the next step higher and make their report to officials of Suxian Prefecture. After the events of the next day, no one was able to unravel this proliferation of reports; their existence and contents remained closely guarded secrets that would ultimately affect the rise and fall of these cadres.

But the string of reports was in fact the last link in the chain of events that culminated in the coordinated armed invasion of Gao Village at noon of October 5, 1997.

The White-Bearded Old Man and the Ruddy-Faced Young Man

After the crackdown on the nonexistent "antitax armed uprising" referred to officially by the authorities as the "Gao Village incident," the old man Gao Zongpeng disappeared. It turned out that he had been taken away by the security forces. After his release, he became a different man, keeping to himself, never uttering a word. Some said he was ill, others said he was nursing his anger and had vowed to bring to justice all the cadres involved in the incident. He disappeared from the village to live the life of a tramp, foraging among dumps; it was rumored that he was scraping together every cent he could muster for a trip to Beijing.

When Gao Zongpeng reappeared in Gao Village, he had already made a trip to Beijing. He said that he had made his way to the Petitions and Appeals Office of the State Council, where he accused the county and township cadres of distorting the facts regarding the Gao Village incident. The trip to Beijing was an eye-opener for Gao Zongpeng. It turned out that he was not the only one who was making complaints about cadres' corruption and the excessive burden on the peasants. From Lingbi County alone many had tried to make the trip to Beijing, but such a journey was a hazardous undertaking indeed. A villager from nearby Huigou County had only gone as far as the next township before word of his plans got out, and he was stopped and taken off the train. The county court could hardly convict him of any crime, so he was sent off to three years' reform through labor. But then there was the woman Yin

Guimei, also of Lingbi County, who had single-handedly made her way to Beijing to seek justice.

Gao Zongpeng was heartened by such comrades. Gao and the woman Yin were taken in hand by the representatives from Lingbi County, who had been summoned to Beijing to deal with their complaints. While in Beijing, those county representatives were all smiles and promises, but once outside the precincts of Beijing and within the jurisdiction of Lingbi County, these creatures changed their tune. Gao and the woman Yin were immediately incarcerated for fifteen days.

Gao Zongpeng would not give up, and vowed to go to Beijing again. And again, pretty much the same thing happened. When he returned from the capital after this second setback, he was the ghost of his old self, his health completely wrecked by the two arduous trips. He feared that he would never be able to make it back to Beijing to let the leaders know the facts of the Gao Village incident. He spent his days in bed, gazing blankly at the ceiling, shaking his head despondently and silently brooding.

One day, unexpectedly, the door to the old man's house was pushed open and in walked a tall young fellow with a ruddy face. It was Zhang Jidong, widely known in the area as a fearless man who always spoke up for the underdog. He was also one of the best- educated among the peasants. Zhang had been accepted into the veterinary department of the Fengyang County campus of Anhui Medical School, but soon his studies were interrupted by the Cultural Revolution and the school itself melted away during the chaos. Zhang received a certificate as a graduate of a "junior professional school" and was sent back to the commune where he came from. First he worked as a veterinarian in Fengmiao Township, but later he started working for a food chain. The business was badly managed and the workers were not paid. Finally, in 1988, Zhang gave up trying to find work and went back to being a peasant. He settled in Dongliu Village, in Lingbi County.

Zhang Jidong soon became known as an expert in making appeals and petitions to the top leadership. He had a way with words. As a student Zhang had written short stories and essays and had even put together a play. Now back in his home county, he was again one of the activists among the peasant writers. A couple of years before, he had written a hundred-thousand-word report based on his investigation of the conditions in his own Dongliu Village regarding the excessive burdens on the peasants and the hostility between peasants and cadres. He mailed the report to the Standing Committee of the People's Consultative Conference in Beijing, and was most pleasantly surprised when his report was published in one of the committee's bulletins. But he was chagrined that his report accomplished nothing and things were going from bad to worse.

For instance, just recently Zhang Jidong with his own eyes had seen Wang Heping, an officer of the township public affairs office, running down the street on market day with a gun in hand, in hot pursuit of a peasant who had refused to pay the excessive per capita tax. When Zhang later took the officer to task for his outrageous behavior, Wang retorted, "I can arrest anybody; I don't need a warrant. I am a graduate of law school."

Zhang said, "No one is above the law."

Wang sneered at this: "Do you really believe that crap you see on TV and read in the newspapers about the rule of law? Don't be daft. Maybe in America a local official can indict the president—but that is America, not China. Let me tell you, this is China, under the rule of man, and I rule over you." Zhang Jidong was shocked that men with such convictions were appointed officials.

The president of the local People's Congress (an honorary

position), Mr. Li Changzhou, was present and heard the exchange and actually took Wang's side. Li said to Zhang, "Now, Zhang, you listen to me. You may agree, or you may not agree, but Wang is telling you the facts as they are. This is China. Let's say you killed a man—you will certainly pay for it with your life. But take me, for instance—if I kill a man, will I die for it? Don't be so sure. Get real; get rid of your one-track mind. I'm telling you this because you are a friend of a relative of mine. Otherwise I wouldn't bother."

Zhang Jidong was flabbergasted; he knew the older man was telling him the truth, but the truth was unacceptable. It was against that background that he heard of the white-bearded old man Gao Zongpeng and his unsuccessful trips to Beijing in search of justice.

Zhang Jidong and Gao Zongpeng clicked immediately when they met. They discussed all the details of the Gao Village incident— the distress of the poor old lady who was only known by her husband's surname and never even had a name of her own, and the villainy of Village Chief Gao Xuewen. They couldn't imagine how the events in the village could have been construed as a violent "antitax uprising." Nor could they imagine how Zheng Jianmin, the deputy head of Fengmiao Township security, relying solely on Gao's distorted version of his visit to Granny Gao's, could have attempted to arrest people and threatened them with a gun. They struggled to comprehend how a handful of township cadres could stage a major attack on a poor village—as the aged Gao Zongpeng had surmised—thus creating one of the gravest cases of miscarriage of justice in the history of Lingbi County. The case weighed heavily on the hearts of the two men. Zhang felt that if the true facts of the case were not thoroughly aired, history could repeat itself in his own village, or any other village. Seeing how the white-bearded old man had almost wrecked his health by his efforts to find justice, Zhang Jidong felt impelled to take up the cause.

The news of Zhang's visit to Gao Zongpeng quickly leaked out, and the township authorities were alarmed. Township Party Boss Hou Chaojie and Zhang Qiwu, the deputy head of township administration, descended on Dongliu Village, and Hou Chaojie came to the point right away, warning Zhang, "You must know that the action taken in Gao Village had been pre-approved by the prefecture and reported to the provincial authorities."

Zhang had not been aware of the fact, but he did not doubt it now that he heard it. Obviously, the Party hack was using his bosses' approval to cover his tracks. The point was, how had the approval been obtained? The township, the county, the prefecture, and even the provincial authorities had been fed false information. And now, in the aftermath of the event, the local officials were trying to preempt complaints by touting the "pre-approval" of their superiors.

Township Party Boss Hou Chaojie ended by warning Zhang Jidong, "Don't you dare meddle in the Gao Village case. Don't even think of going and complaining to higher-ups."

The anxiety that lurked behind Hou's last remark allowed Zhang Jidong to see through their bluff. Realizing that they were afraid of being reported to the central authorities, he retorted, "Since the action was formally approved by the prefecture and had the nod of the provincial leadership, obviously it is correct. So why are you so touchy? It sounds as though something fishy is going on."

Hou Chaojie interrupted him rudely, saying, "You are acting against the local government. If you persist, you will find yourself in deep shit. Don't say you have not been warned."

Then it occurred to Hou Chaojie that it served no purpose to threaten Zhang Jidong, so he changed his tune and said to Zhang, "Don't try to draw firepower to yourself, my man.

Now, look, you have raised complaints regarding affairs in Dongliu Village, your writings have even been published in the bulletin of the National People's Congress. Both the central and the provincial governments ordered investigations in light of your complaints, and the county has opened a special case and conducted a month-long investigation. What did all this fuss amount to? Was anyone punished in the end? No. And now you are agitating again on behalf of the folks in Gao Village. Let's say, for the sake of argument, that this time you win, and we all—from the prefecture to the county down to us at the township—let's say we all lose our jobs. How will it benefit you? Will you be asked to step into our shoes? I don't think so." Finally, in a tone of friendly exhortation, Hou Chaojie said, "You should look up the documents of the Party's Ninth Congress; study it well . . . "

Zhang Jidong was totally confused. Why in the world was Hou bringing up the Party's Ninth Congress. The Ninth Party Congress was in 1969—wasn't that part and parcel of the Cultural Revolution?* Hou was obviously talking through his hat.

After Hou had waddled away, Zhang carefully went over in his mind the whole string of events involved in the Gao Village incident and realized that raising the question again of what really happened, and why, did carry certain risks. It finally dawned on him that to lay bare all the facts of the Gao Village incident would mean making himself an enemy of the local government. But what he couldn't understand was this: Wasn't the local government supposed to stay in step with the central government? Since it was already established that the central

*The Ninth National Congress of the Chinese Communist Party was held in Beijing April 1 to 24, 1969. It has been seen as legitimizing theories and practices of the Cultural Revolution (1966–76); to date there has been no Party document criticizing the conclusions of the Ninth Party Congress.

government—the State Council—was ruling by law, shouldn't the prefecture, the county, as well as the township and village rule their own territory by law as well? Having come to this conclusion, Zhang Jidong came to a painful resolution—he decided to stick his neck out no matter what. And so, in order to get to the bottom of the Gao Village incident he started quietly to carry out an investigation of his own.

Can You Lie to All the People All the Time?

What was to be expected did, after all, take place.

One day, Zhang Jidong was at home in Dongliu Village, sitting idly with a few buddies, when several members of the Fengmiao Township security, in uniform and imposing police caps, burst in, shouting, "Which of you is Zhang Jidong?!" The arrival of these cadres did not bode well for him, but since they did not recognize him, Zhang replied coolly, "He is not in, can we take a message?"

His buddies quickly got the message and immediately fell in with Zhang's ruse, saying, "Please step in. Do sit down. Make yourselves comfortable. Zhang Jidong went to the county town. Would you like to wait, or let us take a message?"

The security men looked around, and said, "All right, when he gets back, tell him to come to the township security." Then they left, not suspecting anything. Zhang Jidong was amused by the scene, but he saw that Party Boss Hou Chaojie was showing his hand and realized that he could no longer stay in Dongliu Village.

Zhang made his way to Si County, where he worked as a migrant laborer to support himself, all the while trying to piece together the facts of the Gao Village incident.

* * *

Party Head Hou Chaojie was not about to give up his vindictive pursuit of Zhang. It was December 26, an icy winter night in the middle of the eleventh month by the lunar calendar, when the head of the township security, Ma Li, and his aide kicked in the door of Zhang's house in Dongliu and burst in. Without showing any legal document pre-approving" their action and without a word of explanation, they dragged Zhang's teenage son, Little Five, from his bed. After hitting and kicking him, they pushed the young fellow out the door, without shoes or warm clothing, and marched him through the open fields until they reached the security headquarters of Huigou Township. By the time they were settled and ready to begin the interrogation, Little Five's teeth were chattering with cold and he was unable to speak a word. Ma Li hoped to squeeze out of Little Five whether his father, Zhang Jidong, was in cahoots with Gao Zongpeng to get to the bottom of the Gao Village incident and see justice done.

The "interrogation" began with Ma Li seizing the young fellow's head and slamming it against the wall. Next the township security chief prodded his mouth with an electric rod, until the boy felt that his head was about to explode. Then Little Five was made to do push-ups on the ice-cold concrete floor while the two interrogators took turns stomping on his ankles. This was just the first round. Next, Ma Li tried a method of his own invention—he used his two thumbs to press down on the two acupressure points on either side of Little Five's eyes, which reduced the young fellow to animal-like screams of pain. A round of martial-arts blows to the chest, enforced by resounding slaps on the cheeks, finished off the first phase of the interrogation. Then Little Five was made to answer the question "Did we hit you?" Little Five was just a raw youth, and was not sure how to act under the circumstances. Not daring to lie, he began to say "You hit me—" Ma Li's fist landed on him and he was beaten until he started moaning, "You didn't hit me . . ." This being unsatisfactory, Ma Li slapped the young fellow hard and ordered, "Louder!" Finally realizing what was required of him Little Five answered, "You did not hit me."

Having softened up the subject to his satisfaction, Ma Li, seeing that it was long past midnight, began the day's real business. He asked Little Five, "Since we didn't hit you or hurt you in any way, then let us be friends. Tell us the truth. Is your father still in league with the white-bearded old man Gao Zongpeng? Is he helping Gao to write letters of accusations?"

Only then did the young fellow realize that, like dogs worrying a bone, they were still chewing over the Gao Village incident—they were still fearful that all the details of the affair would come out one way or another. They did not even dare to hold an interrogation on their own turf but had to sneak into a neighboring township to carry on a surreptitious interrogation.

Little Five was left wondering: The Gao Village incident had taken place in broad daylight and had been witnessed by hundreds of people. How can people's mouths be sealed by threats and arrests? The young fellow could not find an answer to the question: Can you lie to all the people all of the time?

4

THE LONG ROAD

The Cold Shoulder

October 1 is National Day, the celebration of the founding of
the People's Republic of China. October 1, 1994, was the
forty-fifth anniversary of that glorious event, but for Wang
Junbin, a native of Anhui Province holed up in neighboring
Henan, it was not a day of celebration. His heart was chilled
to the core. Home was just a stone's throw away, but he could
not cross the border to return. There was a warrant out for his
arrest.

Two months earlier, on July 30, the Public Security Bureau of
Linquan County, Anhui Province, had distributed a public
notice warning Wang Junbin and his "criminal associates" to
give themselves up. Even though Wang's name was spelled
incorrectly on the warning, he knew that with the distribution
of this public document it was hopeless for him to try to defend
himself. Returning to his native Linquan County would be akin
to diving into a net spread out to catch him. Making things
worse was the fact that following that public warning, the

Linquan County Party Committee announced its decision to expel him from the Party.

His misdemeanor, Wang Jungbin thought to himself, had been to appeal to the Party leadership to implement the Party's own stated policy of relieving the peasants of their excessive burdens. It made no sense that he should be kicked out of the Party. Wang had never imagined that things could come to this pass. Not enough that the peasants were oppressed by poverty; even worse was the psychological pressure they were under. There was so much they wanted to say, to let the world know, but there was no channel for them to express themselves; they had no voice. It was no surprise that in many places the peasants, who are supposed to have "risen to their feet" with the Communist Liberation, were now falling down on their knees to plead for justice. Others, resorting to the ancient desperate practice of "stopping the official's carriage at the risk of death," now threw themselves in front of the cars of Party officials, who are supposed to "cherish them as their own offspring."

Wang Jungbin was only six years old in 1976, when the Cultural Revolution ended, and thus he grew up in an atmosphere where the talk was mostly of reform and opening up, democracy and the rule of law. At the age of eighteen he answered the call of the Party and signed up for the army; while in the army he joined the Party. He grew into a young man who was simultaneously imbued with the spirit of serving the people and acutely conscious of his own rights as an individual. Wang Junbin would never get down on his knees to anyone, nor try to stop an official's car to get his attention. Whatever he had lost, he always had his democratic rights—or so he thought.

He decided to appeal against the public warning issued by the county Party Committee. He was not sure where to direct his appeal. He was aware that a Party organization would usually retain a legal representative in case of lawsuits. When he filled out the form, in the space reserved for "the accused" Wang

Junbin went ahead and wrote the name of the Party secretary of Linquan County, Zhang Xide. He felt he must put down Zhang Xide's name as the accused because the man had played a critical and shameful role in the crackdown that became known as the "Baimiao Township incident" of April 2, 1993. The Baimiao Township incident was not one event but a series of disputes in Wang Village, Baimiao Township, which ultimately led to Wang's name being put on the wanted list. It hardened the ex–army man's resolve to put up a fight.

Linquan County was under the jurisdiction of Fuyang Prefecture, proverbially known as the "Siberia of Anhui Province" for the barrenness of its soil. Situated between two tributaries of the Yangtze River, the area was repeatedly devastated by flood and famine, and still had not experienced a turnaround, in spite of the people's hard work. The tiny flatland county of Linquan must support almost two million people, and is known far and wide as the most populous county in the country. The poverty of the soil and the lack of transportation made this county far and away the poorest. Wang Junbin was born in Baimiao Township, the poorest township in Linquan County.

In the winter of 2001, more than seven years after the events mentioned at the beginning of this narrative, we headed for Baimiao Township. As we made our way through the township, the stark poverty that we saw was absolutely shocking. There were no township enterprises or businesses in sight, and the fields were uniformly planted with scallions and cabbages, the mainstay of the peasants' livelihood. By the time we visited, a road had been paved leading straight to the neighboring province. Huge piles of cabbages and scallions lined the sides of the road, waiting for vegetable dealers to pick up and take to the city to sell. We were shocked by the prices. At 8 yuan to the dollar, and 100 fen to the yuan, a *jin* (slightly over a pound) of scallions was selling for 3 fen, or less than 1 cent. A cartload of fresh scallions would sell for 2 to 3 yuan, or about 31 cents. Cabbages fared slightly better, selling for 10 fen per *jin*. And yet the peasants could not afford to eat their own vegetables. In the village, we saw a man in his thirties squatting in the door of his house and eating a plain bowl of rice, with nothing on it. We asked him why he didn't cook some of his own cabbages to go with his rice. We were heartbroken by his answer: "If I use one *jin* of cabbage, won't I be ten fen short?"

If the township was this poor in 2001, it's hard to imagine what it must have been like more than seven years earlier, in 1993, when the Baimiao Township incident took place. We were told that at the time, the annual per capita income of the peasants was 274 yuan, or a daily income of 80 fen. Yet in spite of the abject poverty, taxes and demands for payments kept piling in from the county, the township, and the village. The peasants were reduced to the proverbial state: "boiling with anger, but afraid to speak."

The Baimiao Township incident was first ignited over an unrelated case of bullying by the Party boss of Wang Village in the fall of 1993. Wang Junbin had a friend, Wang Hongchao, and Wang Hongchao, being a shrewd young fellow, realized that it was impossible to make a living by farming alone, so he joined his father-in-law selling rat poison in the area. Between the two of them they made a tolerable income, by local standards. One day, just as young Wang Hongchao was out on one of his rounds, the village Party boss, Gao Jianjun, heading a so-called tax-enforcement shock team, came to his house and demanded a payment of 6 yuan toward work on the school building. There was nothing wrong with the school building at the time, and Wang's mother didn't have 6 yuan handy. She said to Gao, "My son is not at home. Come by some other day." Hardly were the words were out of her mouth than Party Boss Gao and his gang made off with the family's TV set. Wang's mother was completely shocked and could only stutter, "How can you do this? How— How—?" The two families were slightly related, and the old woman never imagined that Gao could abuse his relatives like that. But Gao, totally unmoved, walked away with the TV set.

Wang Hongchao was furious when he heard what had happened. He decided that something must be done about this lawless taxing and extortion going on in the village. He met up with his friend the army veteran Wang Junbin and a mutual friend of theirs, Wang Xiangdong. The three young men talked over the situation and decided that the sensible thing was to go to the township for a just ruling on the case. They were doing nothing wrong, they figured, by going to the next level of the Party leadership. It was their legal right, they assumed.

So the three young men from Wang Village went to the township center and looked up the township Party boss, Han Chunsheng. It was a day they would always remember— October 28, 1993. It was the day when these three young men for the first time got a good dose of the bureaucratic runaround, and were chilled to the bone by what they experienced. Han made it clear that he would do nothing on their behalf.

Knowing that he was being shielded by his superior at the township level, Village Party Boss Gao Jianjun became all the more insolent. When he learned that Wang Hongchao and his friends had gone to the township to accuse him of snatching a TV, Gao strode to Wang's house again and made off with his bicycle. But to be robbed of a TV and a bike because of nonpayment of an unjustified tax of 6 yuan was more than the long-suffering peasants of Wang village could put up with. They decided that enough was enough. They came forward one after another and showed the three young men solid proofs of endless cases of forced payments, unjustified collection of "village cash reserves," lawless fines, and other official swindles.

On our own visit to the village, we had a chance to inspect three copies of such evidence. On a copy of a "peasant tax and payments card" stamped with an official seal we saw clear traces of changes in the record of figures for the amount of land under contract. The figures grew imperceptibly, and it goes without saying that taxes grew in proportion. On the records of payment for the "village cash reserve" and the "township combined payments," the changes were even more confusing. For instance, altogether there were fourteen items for these two categories, but what each item stood for was never explained. Among all this confusion, one thing was clear: one card recorded what the peasants were made to pay, and the other recorded a lower figure, for the benefit of the inspectors. Basically, double books were kept.

Armed with these solid proofs of excessive taxation of the peasants and illegal record keeping, the three friends Wang Junbin, Wang Hongchao, and Wang Xiangdong resolved to appeal to the higher authorities. Having had a taste of the cold shoulder at the township level, they decided to go one step higher—to Linquan County.

They were shocked to get an equally cold reception at the county level. They now demanded to see the Party secretary of the county himself. This man was the highest representative of the Party for the whole county. He would never tolerate violations of Party policy at the grassroots level, the three young men thought to themselves.

"We want to see Comrade Zhang Xide," they announced quietly to the receptionist.

The man behind the desk cast a look in their direction. Seeing three unsophisticated peasants, he asked, visibly annoyed, "Do you know whom you are asking for?'

"Of course. The county Party secretary!"

"And who may you be?"

"We are from Wang Village, Baimiao Township."

The man said contemptuously, "So the county Party secretary wants to see the likes of you? Go to the township for affairs of your village."

"We did. But the township didn't care."

"They didn't care, so you come to us? Supposing everybody acted like you, rushing to the county Party secretary for all your petty affairs? How do you think the secretary can carry on his work?"

The three young men were stunned.

Of the three friends, Wang Xiangdong was the one with the shortest fuse. "The township doesn't give a damn," he said. "If we don't call on county leaders, which way should we turn?"

The man behind the desk stood up, opened his arms wide, and started shooing them off, saying, "Out. Out. Out. We are busy here!"

Wang Hongchao, who had been standing quietly aside, now stated calmly, "We are asking the county Party leadership to implement the Party Central's policy of relieving the peasants of their excessive burden."

"Then go and deal with whoever refuses to relieve your burden" was the retort.

"We absolutely need to talk to Comrade Zhang Xide." Wang Hongchao repeated firmly.

"The answer is no!"

"Why not?"

"I say no, and I mean no!" The man left no room for negotiation.

Wang Hongchao, still not giving up, said, "Is this your attitude toward the people?"

"Beat it," the other said disdainfully, "or you'll see worse."

When the three young men came out of the Party Committee building, their faces were blank. The strongest belief in their young hearts had been painfully crushed. When they returned and told their story, the villagers decided that three people could not make enough of a show to catch the leadership's attention. If three hundred people turned out, in a dozen trucks and tractors, it would be different. Soon a convoy of peasants was rumbling into the county town. But that show of numbers only aggravated the situation. The county leaders regarded the villagers' action as ganging up to raise hell.

After these rebuffs, the villagers decided that their problem of overtaxation could not be solved in Linquan County. There were three choices left: appeal to authorities at the prefecture level, appeal to the provincial authorities, or go to Beijing. The villagers had their doubts about the first two choices. The officials at these various regional levels were linked in such a mesh of relationships, it was inevitable that they would shield each other. Newspapers, radio broadcasts, and TV programs were all full of stories of peasants' accusations and appeals to higher officials being relayed downward tier by tier until they ended up in the very hands of the original targets of the complaints.

The people of Wang village deliberated back and forth. Eventually they concluded that the only workable solution was to go directly to Beijing, to appeal to the Party Central Committee and to petition the central government. It was, after all, the Party Central and the central government that had laid down the new policies about reducing the peasants' burden. The villagers figured that only the top levels of authority cared about them.

Of course the villagers realized that making an appeal to the center and going over the heads of one's direct superiors involved certain risks. Bringing problems in the village and township directly to the Party Central was in effect making accusations against the county leaders; it could even be seen as smearing them, tantamount to saying that the Linquan County leadership was not doing its job. The villagers were pretty sure that County Party Secretary Zhang Xide would never let them get away with it.

This Zhang Xide was quite a celebrity. He was often seen on local TV making public speeches, his hands sweeping through the air to emphasize a point. His speeches were obviously drafted by his assistant. The minute he departed from the script, coarse jokes and barbarous obscenities would take over. On one occasion, when he was talking about enforcement of the one-child policy, he raised a clenched fist and announced, "I'd rather see seven grave mounds than one extra birth," obviously referring to women who died from botched abortions. This shocking saying of Zhang Xide's was whispered far and wide, chilling everyone who heard it.

Going to Beijing meant being on the wrong side of Zhang Xide. Who was willing to take the risk, the villagers wondered. Who was capable of shouldering such a responsibility? All eyes fell on the ex-army man Wang Junbin, the peddler Wang Hongchao, and the smart young fellow Wang Xiangdong, the only three people from the village who were young and educated.

A Touch of Warmth: The First Trip to Beijing

Almost two months after the three friends' first brush with authority over the 6-yuan school-building tax and the forcible removable of Wang Hongchao's TV and bicycle, back in the fall of 1993, the three friends made ready to leave for Beijing, bearing written evidence of overtaxation safely in their pockets.

When Wang Junbin and his friends got off the train and were actually standing on the platform of Beijing railway station, they were seized with emotion. They felt as if they were being folded into their mother's bosom. They couldn't help wishing they could visit Tiananmen Square and the Great Hall of the People and the vermilion walls of Zhongnanhai, the headquarters of the Party Central Committee, and other emblems of the Party state. But they could not afford to indulge their personal enthusiasms. The villagers had squeezed themselves to put up the money for their trip and they must set out immediately on the business that they had been entrusted with. They asked for road directions to the Petitions and Appeals Office of the Central Committee and to that of the State Council (each maintained its own such office).

Contrary to their expectations, things went very smoothly at the reception. The response to their petition was so swift and favorable that the three were actually quite flustered. The comrades listened to their list of complaints and promised to write directly to the Anhui provincial units concerned, to request an investigation and satisfactory resolution to their problem. It was bitterly cold in Beijing, the wind cutting like daggers into their bones, but the three young men felt suffused with the warmth of their reception.

Wang Hongchao suggested that since they were here, they should look up all the government institutions concerned, to get the most out of this trip on behalf of the villagers. So the three friends asked their way to the Ministry of Agriculture.

At the Ministry of Agriculture, they felt perfectly at home and laid bare their case. The comrades there listened carefully, looked at the documents, and unequivocally stated that officials at Baimiao Township and Wang Village were in the wrong. Without being asked, they wrote a letter of support which they asked Wang and his friends to take to the Anhui provincial Agricultural Committee. The letter was a printed form with a space to jot down some general remarks. But on this occasion, the comrades wrote down the details of the case and added an admonishment: "This kind of extortion is in direct violation of the stated policies of the Party and the government regarding relieving the peasants of their excessive burden . . ." At the end of the letter, instead of the perfunctory "Hoping you will look to the matter" etc., this letter added: "Now we are sending them to you; please make sure you look into their case and deal with it conscientiously." The comrades at the Ministry of Agriculture saw Wang Junbin and his friends all the way to the gate. Before saying good-bye, one of the comrades said with a sigh, "The leadership has again and again sent down directives, but at the grass roots the cadres are perfectly heedless." Such concern sounded sincere and warming to the hearts of the three innocent young peasants.

The weather in Beijing was windless and clear, but the piercing cold sunk its teeth into their skin mercilessly. As the train headed south, the temperature rose perceptibly. But for Wang Junbin and his friends, the nearer to home they got, the colder they felt. After this, their first visit to Beijing, they felt more and more alienated from their native place. As they approached home, they were actually gripped by fear.

On the other hand, as they left Beijing, the three young men's excitement at their favorable reception was also tinged with bitterness, clouding their good mood. They realized that as good as Beijing was, it did not belong to them, and they did not belong in Beijing. They were, after all, strangers here. They were tied to Wang Village, Baimiao Township, Linquan County. Their fates were controlled by people down there, in the hands of puny creatures from the village or township. No matter how far they traveled, those hands still held the strings.

Once across the Yangtze River, the three men were silent,

each lost in his own thoughts. All night they nodded to the rumblings and clanging of the train and did not sleep a wink. At daybreak, they were tired and sleepy, but the train had stopped and they found themselves in Hefei, the provincial capital.

Once in Hefei, the three followed the instructions of the comrades at the Ministry of Agriculture and headed immediately for the Anhui office of the "leading group for relieving peasants' burdens." The comrades at the Peasants' Burden Relief Office listened carefully to the complaints of the three Wangs, acknowledged that they had a case, and proceeded immediately to write a letter to their subordinates at the corresponding office on a lower tier—the Peasants' Burden Relief Office of Linquan County. The cadre did not mince words: "We have received peasants from Baimiao Township of your county, directed to us by the Ministry of Agriculture. From the records that they showed, there is a grave problem of excessive taxation. According to our information, the three petitioners have repeatedly appealed to your leadership, but with no results, and popular resentment is widespread. We now relay to you the position of the Ministry of Agriculture, as laid out in their letter, which we enclose with other related material. We hope you will speedily send personnel to make a thorough investigation and deal with it appropriately. If the peasants have been unduly taxed, it is imperative to make compensation. Please make a report of your handling of the case . . . "

To make sure that there was no misunderstanding, the comrades at the provincial level carefully stamped the letter with an official seal. Before seeing the peasants off, the comrades gave them a copy of a pamphlet listing the various Party policies regarding relieving the peasants' burden, which they themselves had compiled. As the three young peasants left the building, they looked back gratefully at the rundown building that housed the provincial Peasants' Burden Relief Office. During this stop in Hefei, the three young men also looked up the

Disciplinary Committee of the Anhui Party organization. The comrades at the provincial Disciplinary Committee also assured them that they would look into the matter.

After their return home, Wang Junbin, Wang Hongchao, and Wang Xiangdong once again walked into the office of the Party Committee of Linquan County. They took out the letters, one given them by the Ministry of Agriculture and one given to them by the Anhui provincial Peasants' Burden Relief Office. This time the office personnel did not shoo them out.

It was obvious that the county office had already received word directly from Beijing. It could be safely assumed that County Party Secretary Zhang Xide was by now well aware that the peasants from Wang Village had gone all the way to Beijing to make accusations against him. He emerged from his office, his face creased with smiles, and immediately sat down to write a note, directed to the Baimiao Township Party Committee and township administration. The note read: "Peasants from Wang village have complained to the higher authorities demanding the return of money paid over and above the mandatory figure for cash reserve. Please deal with this properly and in a timely fashion, and return in full the money owing."

The three men took the note and scrutinized it. It was a hastily handwritten scrawl, and it took the three some time to make out the words. When they did make out the writing, the wording left them perplexed. How would "the mandatory figure for cash reserve" be defined? Why not deal with the issue officially as the comrades did at the central and the provincial level? Why not point out the gravity of the issue? How to account for the fact that the peasants had repeatedly gone to the township and county and been rebuffed? Despite these unanswered questions, it was indeed a personal handwritten note from the county Party Secretary, promising to return the excessive payments extorted from them. The three months between the fall of 1993, when the three men first decided to make appeals to Beijing, and now, when they held Zhang Xide's note in their hands, had not been spent in vain. The peasants of Wang village were overjoyed.

One can imagine the mixed feelings of the township and village cadres as they were handed the note from County Party Boss Zhang Xide. By sending them this note through the three peasant representatives, Zhang as good as reproached them for letting him down and bringing trouble on his head. On the other hand, they figured, it was but a note scribbled on a scrap of paper. On second reading, the wording of the note—such as saying that "peasants . . . have complained . . . "—smacked of Zhang Xide's own resentment. Moreover, Zhang's final exhortation, "Please deal with this properly," was as good as telling them that he was washing his hands of the matter.

In spite of whatever underhanded insinuations might be hidden in the note, Baimiao Township officials had to make some gestures toward resolving the problem of the peasants' excessive burden. Under the supervision of the county Party Disciplinary Committee, an investigative group was set up that included peasant representatives and started work in the township and the village. The problems were so obvious, it took no more than an initial examination to find in excess of 11,000 yuan extorted for the "village cash reserve" for the year 1993. In auditing the records of Wang Village, the peasant representatives came across mountains of unjustified IOU notes for cash, as well as unexplained withdrawals from the village cash reserve and other public monies. Sometimes the figures for withdrawals from the accounts of township and village public funds were lumped together. Separate withdrawals for the year

1993 were for as much as 47,650 yuan, but the record was made out as 33,760.46 yuan. So where had the extra 13,883.54 yuan gone? The peasants were furious at the messed-up state of the village finances. Meanwhile, two months passed after County Party Secretary Zhang Xide wrote his note, and still the cadres made only token payments to the villagers.

Moreover, strange things were taking place which were very unsettling. First of all, Wang Junbin, who had always worked for the township land control office, was suddenly fired. After that, his friends Wang Hongchao and Wang Xiangdong received a summons from the township administrative office. The minute they walked into the building compound, each got a sound beating from thugs who lay in waiting.

By the spring of 1994, the peasants of Wang village found themselves in a situation where small amounts of repayment for excessive taxation was merely symbolic. Meanwhile they were made to feel the full weight of retaliation for making accusations and trying to get repayment. Something had to be done about it. In desperation the peasants of Wang village again gathered, all three hundred strong, and went to the county headquarters demanding repayment according to Zhang Xide's own note.

In taking this step the peasants once again showed their ignorance—or perhaps it was naïveté—if they expected an official to keep his word. Zhang Xide flew into a temper the minute he saw the crowd. Without a word about his handwritten note promising repayment, he announced, "Go ahead and raise hell. I am not lifting a finger to solve your problems!"

The peasants asked, "Is this the spirit of the Party's policies?"

This further provoked Zhang, who shouted, "Well, go to Beijing, if you can!"

But they had already been to Beijing. Now, the peasants figured, it was up to the county to implement the policies handed down from Beijing, especially as there were letters of instructions concerning their case. Why go again? It was now up to the county Party boss to take action.

But Zhang had totally lost his cool. "Go ahead and raise hell," he shouted. "The more chaos the better! Just wait till I deal with you!"

The peasants, at a loss, turned to the county's Party Disciplinary Committee, the entity that originally had sent out investigative groups of its own and had uncovered many problems in the "village cash reserve." Now, on hearing the peasants' complaints, the head of the Disciplinary Committee shrugged. "I told them to pay back the excessive charges. But they just won't. What do you want me to do?" The county Party boss would not implement policy and the Disciplinary Committee could not, or would not, enforce discipline to make the county boss act.

Things were again at an impasse. As the villagers seethed in anger, Wang Junbin, Wang Hongchao, and Wang Xiangdong decided that they would see the struggle through to the bitter end. To them the problem was implementing Party policy and relieving the peasants' burden pure and simple. They never imagined that things could be twisted by the county bosses to fit their own political agenda.

After that fruitless call on Zhang Xide, back at the village things took a downward turn for the peasants. Wang Hongchao got hold of an astounding piece of news. He had a relative, Shi Canzhou, who was the political director of the Baimiao Township Security Station. Shi took him aside one day and said, "Don't get involved in making any more accusations to the higher-ups. Arrests are being planned. Be on guard." It was the thirtieth of March, 1994, roughly two months after County Party boss Zhang Xide had written his note. Wang Hongchao was shocked at Shi's tip-off. He quickly rushed to tell his pals

Wang Junbin and Wang Xiangdong, and soon the whole village was alerted. Terror seized the villagers. They organized a night patrol, and Wang Hongchao actually succeeded in getting his hands on the village broadcasting set and spiriting it away into his own house, so that he could alert the rest of the village if anything happened. The villagers felt themselves prepared for the worst, but they were still shocked at how quickly the worst happened.

Heaven Above and the Emperor Beyond

It was April 2, 1994, and past eleven o'clock at night—nothing special for city folk, but late for the people in Wang Village, who were all tucked in their bedrolls, fast asleep. At this unearthly hour, a van crept stealthily into the village. The van parked at the west end of the village, and five men alighted. Later on it was disclosed that they were from the Baimiao township security station: Shi Canzhou, the security officer who had dropped the warning; two policemen, Wang and Zhang; and two security hirelings, Wang and Liu. They crept noiselessly into the village. But the night patrol man saw their approach and followed them undetected. He saw the five men poke around the houses of those who had stuck their necks out to make petitions, and even push against their doors to see if they were secured. The patrol ran toward Wang Hongchao's place, shouting, "There are strange men in the village!" Wang Hongchao's sister-in-law happened to be visiting with them. A light sleeper, she jumped up from her bed, rushed to the room where the broadcasting set was stored, turned it on, and shouted at the top of her lungs, "Thief! Thief! Good neighbors, out with your rakes, out with your poles. Don't let them escape!" In the silence of the night, the call went out clearly over the whole village. Men, women, and children were all alerted.

The sudden commotion shocked the interlopers. Now that they had been discovered, the two security guys were frightened and took flight. These hirelings were especially hated by the villagers: the regular policemen could in some sense be said to be doing their jobs, but these irregulars were considered outright collaborators and mercenaries and would be soundly beaten if caught. Political Director Shi Canzhou, finding himself exposed, turned and stumbled away in the dark, leaving the van behind. The two policemen, Wang and Zhang, and the driver, did not move quickly enough, were separated in the dark, and were taken by the villagers.

The villagers asked each man in isolation from the others: "Where are you from? What are you doing here?"

One policeman said, "We are from Tile-Roof Inn Village . . . "

The other policeman said, "We are from Yellow Ridge Village."

The driver said, "We are from the silk factory in town. Our boss is here to discuss some business."

The three contradictory answers gave rise to more suspicions.

The fact was, Wang Village, Linquan County, was situated on the border of Anhui and Henan provinces. A footpath by the house of the village schoolmaster was actually the border between the two provinces. There is a saying that when the schoolmaster's little son peed on the path, he was actually irrigating the lands of two provinces. Situated in such a precarious position, with three men in police uniforms prowling in the village in the dark of night, the villagers were naturally alarmed. They asked the men to produce their IDs. They refused and broke away, but they were on unfamiliar terrain. Seeing the villagers hard on their heels, one of the policemen stopped running and took out his gun. "Stop, or I'll fire!" he hollered. The villagers, having the advantage of number, were not intimidated. It just confirmed their suspicion that the three, with their contradictory stories, were up to no good. Why not show their IDs? Why run away, leaving their van behind?

Convinced that their uniforms were fake, they villagers gave the three interlopers a sound beating.

Under this assault, the driver blurted out the truth: "They really are policemen from the township police station. They have given me 10 yuan for the use of my van, and a pack of cigarettes, and they are here to arrest people." He took out the 10-yuan note and the pack of cigarettes, hoping to be let go. The villagers turned to the two policemen, Zhang and Wang, who finally confessed that they were indeed from Baimiao Township, and were here to make arrests.

This information merely led to more questions:

"Arresting our representatives?"

"Why not do it openly?"

"Why pretend to be from Tile-Roof Inn and Yellow Ridge villages and the silk factory in town?"

"Why try to run away?"

The villagers insisted on getting answers.

One of the policemen said, in a small voice, "We are here to check on gambling . . . "

The other said, "We are here on patrol . . . "

This was really far-fetched. For the previous forty-five years—since the Communist Liberation—the township police force had never once done any patrolling in the villages. Why now, just when the villagers had been repaid some of the excessive taxes, should they suddenly show up on patrol? And why, in particular, were they conducting their so-called patrolling right at the doorsteps of the village representatives? The villagers soon discovered that one of the policemen had been drinking. Knowing that their sort was capable of anything and were no better than street thugs when under the influence of alcohol, the villagers took away the gun and the four sets of handcuffs that the men had with them. It was now clear that they were indeed here to make four secret arrests, and that their targets were none other than Wang Junbin, Wang Xiangdong, Wang Hongchao, and another young man, Wang Hongqin.

The villagers were furious, shouting at the policemen: "When we were beaten, you looked the other way. Now that we have appealed to the central leadership, you try secretly to arrest us! Aren't you ashamed of yourselves?" They were so angry that they smashed the van. The policeman Wang and the driver soon made off. As for the drunken policeman Zhang, he was quickly sobered by the turn of events and fled. As far as the villagers were concerned, that was the end of the matter.

That's what transpired during the night of April 2, 1994. It was a molehill of a local fracas that the county Party bosses later tried to turn into a mountain, an insurrection in which township policemen were attacked and guns were stolen. The drunken policeman Zhang later claimed that he had been seriously injured in the fight.

Following the flight of the three intruders, one villager gathered together the gun, cartridges, and the handcuffs that had been taken from the two policemen and handed them over to the head of the township militia, Wang Dongliang, who happened to be a resident of Wang Village. By this time it was already into the small hours of the morning, and the villagers trouped home to catch some sleep.

No one could have imagined that by the next morning, when the county Party Secretary Zhang Xide learned what had happened, the story of the night's event would be totally distorted. Despite the fact that the two policemen, two security guards (who had fled at the first sign of trouble), and the conscripted driver had all gone free and the gun, cartridges, and handcuffs had all been safely returned to official custody, the Linquan County Party Committee, headed by its boss, Zhang Xide, made a false report to his superiors at the prefecture level and launched an unprecedentedly bloody campaign against the villagers, putatively to "rescue kidnapped policemen and search for guns in Wang Village."

The following morning, April 3, 1994, a police detail numbering more than a hundred armed men started off from the county seat in eight police vans, with sirens heralding their approach. The cars were fitted with machine guns and the men were armed with helmets and bullet-proof vests and sported police batons and shields in their hands. As the convoy entered Wang village, its loudspeaker blared the order "No one is to leave!" But these policemen had forgotten, or never knew, that the village straddled the border between Anhui and Henan. All the residents had to do was to walk to the edge of the village to find themselves in Henan Province, out of the reach of the Anhui police, and this is just what many of them did. Of course there were many who stayed put: old people, or those who had never joined in making petitions, or outsiders visiting relatives—all felt safe and saw no need to join the crowd now streaming into Henan Province. Much to their surprise, however, the invading armed police made no distinction between men, women, and children, residents and outsiders, and gave a vicious beating to everyone they could lay their hands on. The village echoed to the sounds of curses, kicks and blows, the shattering of household utensils, the screams of children, the protests of adults, as well as the screeches of roosters flying up to the rooftops, the barking of dogs jumping over the wall, and the thud of pigs battering against their pens in panic.

Obviously, the targets of this surprise attack were the people who had gone to the higher authorities to make appeals. These people's homes were ransacked, pots and pans were smashed, and even chimneys were knocked over. A collection of twenty silver dollars that Wang Hongqin had treasured, 700 yuan that Wang Xiangdong had saved, and a gramophone of Wang Hongchao's—all disappeared in the raid. The invaders took eight thousand tubes of rat poison, Wang Hongchao's whole inventory, and emptied the contents into his wheat storage. After stirring the poison in vigorously with a spade, they left in triumph. The twelve people who were arrested in the raid of April 3, 1994, were mostly people who had had nothing to do with making petitions: old men, young women on visits with relatives, and even students who had crossed over from neighboring Henan province.

In the aftermath of the attack, the authorities of Linquan County issued a public letter, claiming that the action taken on April 3 was "correct and timely," "in accordance with the law," and "supported by their superiors" and that there should be no "murmurs against the action" and so on and so forth.

Seven years later, in 2001, we were able to interview one of the arrested, Wang Yongming, a law-abiding peasant who had been minding his own business, and even was a member of the village committee. When the police arrived, he was busy repairing the pig pen and was not at all concerned, feeling that he was the last person in the village with any reason to be alarmed at the appearance of the police. So Wang Yongming was stunned when two policemen stopped in front of him and hustled him into a police van without so much as a by-your-leave.

Wang Yongming and the other detainees, all with their hands bound behind their backs, were taken to the Baimiao Township security station, where they all were beaten. One of the detainees had ventured to protest, and was punished by having boiling water poured over his head. Soon, the detainees were moved to the Linquan County detention center. As they got out of the police van, they were kicked into a kneeling position and whipped with braided cable wires. After the whipping, they were shackled and made to run three rounds in the yard, with whips urging them on. Later they had to pay 7 yuan each for the use of the shackles. That same night, the detainees were all hustled into a cell, where Wang Yongming endured more agony when boot-shod policemen stepped on his hand. After two days of detention, inexplicably, Wang Yongming was moved in with death row inmates, who in their own sadistic fury and despair beat him, tore at his hair, knocked his head against the wall, and tortured him in every possible way. The guards looked on nonchalantly.

Wang Yongming was incarcerated for eight days and then kicked out—he not only got no explanation, but was actually forced to pay a fee toward his keep during his wrongful imprisonment! As a parting shot he was told, "No blabbing, mind you!" Seven years had passed since then, but the marks of the bruises left by the shackles were still clearly visible on his ankles. Thus the Linquan County authorities' swift crackdown on what they referred to as the "Baimiao Township incident."

The Clandestine Trips to Beijing

Most of the peasants who had crossed the border into Henan to avoid arrest were too scared to return to their village, and eked out a living as migrants. The hardier ones ventured back by night, only to find their fields untended and their households looted of their few pitiful possessions during their absence.

One day the village representatives—Wang Junbin (the army veteran), Wang Xiangdong, Wang Hongchao, and Wang Hongqin, who had all been in hiding in Henan Province—managed to elude the spies from their own county and got together to confer. Reviewing the situation, the four men decided that they had no choice but to report the facts of the crackdown on the so-called "Baimiao Township incident" to the Party Central Committee in Beijing. It was decided that Wang Junbin would stay behind to keep an eye on things, while Wang Hongchao, Wang Xiangdong, and Wang Hongqin hopped on a bus to Zhengzhou, the Henan provincial capital, whence they could catch the train to Beijing.

It was Wang Hongchao's and Wang Xiangdong's second trip to Beijing. On their arrival the three made a beeline for the Petitions and Appeals Offices of the Party Central Committee and the State Council, situated near the Yongdingmen Railway Station. But when they got there whom should they find lying in ambush for them but security officers from their own home county, who immediately pounced on them. The three men were dragged away, furiously denying the false accusations, but once having fallen into the hands of their own county security, they were helpless. The security officers promptly hauled them back to Anhui Province, where they were accused of snatching two handguns and fifteen cartridges from the police and planning an attack on Beijing itself. They were taken not to their native Linquan County but to Taihe County, the home of the Linquan County Party boss, Zhang Xide, their nemesis and the hand behind this illegal arrest.

In Taihe County, Wang Hongchao and his two companions were detained and tortured for two months, a painful, humiliating, and terrifying experience beyond imagination. Their hands were tied behind their backs twenty-four hours a day. To eat they had to get down to their knees and lick from the bowl set before them. At the call of nature, they were forced to pull down their pants with their manacled hands and relieve themselves as best they could. At night they could only lie on their sides, their bodies crushing one arm or the other. The punishment was designed to strip them of all human dignity, to make them lose all power of thinking, and turn them into passive creatures at the beck and call of their masters—while also transforming them into brutalized dogs who would attack on their masters' orders.

Through the summer of 1994, Wang Hongchao, Wang Xiangdong, and Wang Hongqin languished in detention and the army veteran Wang Junbin bided his time in Henan, unaware of what had happened to his friends. Then there was an unexpected turn of events: Yu Guangxuan, who held the honorary post of vice president of the Linquan County People's Consultative Conference,* got word of what had gone down in Wang Village—from the peasants' trip to Beijing, to Zhang Xide's "repayment" letter, to the foiled clandestine police action on the night of April 2, to the crackdown on the following day, to the illegal arrests in Beijing and the secret detention in Taihe County. It was a clear case of taking revenge on the peasants for making appeals and petitions. Yu Guangxuan decided he was not going to stand by with his hands folded and let the situation continue.

One Sunday, he took a bus to neighboring Xincai County, in Henan, found a post office, and sent off a telegram to General Secretary Jiang Zemin, in which he detailed the facts in the Baimiao Township incident. The cost of the long telegram was equivalent to two months' household expenses for Vice President Yu. Of course the post office personnel at Xincai understood the momentous implications of sending such a telegram, but as the story did not pertain to their own locality, there was no risk, so it was dispatched straight to Beijing.

Vice President Yu of the county People's Consultative Conference later found out how, after arriving Beijing, his telegram made the usual trip up the bureaucratic ladder to the top, and then downward step by step until it landed back in the hands of Linquan County's own Party boss, Zhang Xide.

Zhang was furious, and ordered an immediate investigation

* The Chinese People's Political Consultative Conference, abbreviated CPPCC, is a political advisory body consisting of both Party and non-Party members, who are representatives of different segments of the population, and advise the Party and the government on policies.

as to who had sent that telegram. The job was not as easy as one might imagine. The fact was, when Yu Guangxuan sent the telegram he had anticipated just such an outcome, and did not sign his own name but instead signed himself "Wang Hongqin." Of course, according to the investigators whoever had sent the telegram could not be Wang Hongqin, because he was languishing in detention in Taihe County jail, with his hands manacled behind his back twenty-four hours a day. So Wang was the first to be eliminated from the list of suspects. In order to further confuse the issue, the vice President had added the phrase "retired cadre" to the name Wang Hongqin. In vain did Zhang Xide's henchmen comb the population of Wang Village—they could not find a single retired cadre named Wang or otherwise. But they found a retired worker Wang Hongzhang. Even though a retired cadre was a world apart from a retired worker, and the last characters for the names were different, still it was good enough for the Linquan County public security. One day, Wang Hongzhang was told to report at his work unit. He had been owed his pension for a long time, so Wang went forth cheerfully, expecting to be paid. The minute he walked in the door, county security seized him. Poor Wang Hongzhang had no idea what they were talking about when they asked him about a telegram, but his denials only elicited beatings.

This unexpected arrest gave rise to a further twist in the unfolding comedy of errors: the unintended effect of rousing another man who heretofore had not concerned himself with village affairs so far, Wang Hongling. During the police raid of April 3, Wang Hongling's wife had been arrested and shackled like the rest. His brother, Wang Hongbin, who tried to defend his sister-in-law, had been poked with an electric prod and seriously hurt. And now here was Wang Hongzhang, wrongfully arrested for something he'd had nothing to do with. The thing was, Wang Hongling, Wang Hongbin and Wang Hongzhang were all brothers who would die for each other. Wang Hongling worked at a job in Henan County. With one brother still recovering from a brutal beating and the other brother under wrongful arrest, Wang Hongling had had enough. He decided to do something not only for his brothers but for all his compatriots in Wang Village. He gave up his well-paid job and looked up Wang Junbin, the army veteran still in hiding in Henan. The two men teamed up together and successfully recruited fifty-six peasants from Wang Village. This group made its way to Beijing in June of 1994. It was the third attempt of the peasants of Wang Village to get their message out and see justice done.

Linquan County Party Boss Zhang Xide was extremely alarmed when heard about the trip and immediately took action to counter its effects. He sent a hundred-man "work team" of local cadres into Wang Village who made a great show of going to solve problems. Members of the work team ate and drank at the expense of the peasants and went around the village with loudspeakers issuing propaganda reminiscent of the days of the Cultural Revolution. It was an unbearable affliction to the already hard-up villagers, not to mention the "work team's" true purpose, which was to appear to make moot the objective of the planned third trip. To add to their misery, there was a drought that summer.

As the fifty-six peasants led by Wang Junbin and Wang Hongling filtered back from this third, and unsuccessful, trip to Beijing, they could not tend their parched fields because of the interference of the work teams. After the hundred-man work team, Zhang Xide sent in a two-hundred-strong shock team in thirty cars and trucks. They surrounded the village and announced that the county would soon hold a mass meeting of ten thousand people, to educate the peasants on the issue of making appeals to Beijing. An atmosphere of fear was pervasive. Some people left the land altogether, and more than a thousand *mu* of corn was lost. So oppressive was the witch-hunt atmosphere that a peasant called Wang Yang, who had joined the group of fifty-six on the villagers' third trip to Beijing, overcome with fear, took poison one night and died.

In October of the same year, the security station of Linquan County issued a public notice calling on Wang Junbin and his companions to give themselves up as "criminals" wanted by the police for "illegally detaining police," "robbery," and disseminating "reactionary propaganda." A public warning was issued to their families as well. This was followed by a public notice from the county Party organization announcing the expulsion of Wang Junbin from the Party—the event with which our story began.

When Men Fear Not Death, What Hold Do You Have over Them?

Running parallel to the action taken against Wang Junbin, who had led the third fruitless trip to Beijing, the next step taken by Linquan County in retaliation for the peasants' repeated appeals to Beijing was a public trial of Wang Xiangdong and Wang Hongchao, two of the three men who had been dragged back from Beijing and thrown into the Taihe County jail. On the day of the trial the authorities posted police and plainclothesmen all over the place, but that did not prevent nearly seven hundred peasants from far and near from attending the trial to see what evidence the court could produce against their trusted representatives.

The public prosecutor proceeded to read out the "vicious crimes" of Wang Xiangdong and Wang Hongchao, as well as evidence they had collected in the village. The villagers—who didn't give a hoot about maintaining order in the kangaroo court—started shouting.

"Lies! False evidence!"

"These good men have been wronged!"

"Release them immediately!"

"You are the ones to be tried."

The public trial descended into complete chaos.

It was unheard of in the area that a crowd could hijack a court of law. The judge and the court police were completely at a loss as to how to react. When men fear not death, what hold do you have over them? The fully armed court police were afraid of things getting out of control, and snuck away. The judge had no choice but to announce that the trial would be deferred to another day. But to open the trial again would be asking for another such demonstration from the massed peasants. To save face, the county court surreptitiously found both men guilty of "obstructing official business" and sentenced Wang Xiangdong to two years in prison and Wang Hongchao to one year in prison with two years probation.

Wang Hongchao was forced to serve seven months of his sentence before being released on probation. Since the Baimiao Township incident of April 2, 1994, the previous year, he had been either hiding in Henan, or on the road to Beijing, or in jail. He was in the dark as to what had happened to the village and his own home in the intervening time. Now he finally returned to see his ransacked home, and his rat poison mixed with his wheat stores. His wife was losing her mind from the family disasters and his only daughter suffered from hallucinations and had had to quit school. Stunned by the situation facing him, Wang remembered the saying, "From time immemorial, the peasants turned to authority for justice; if that fails, what can hold them back?" Indeed, Wang Hongchao thought back to their second trip to Beijing, when he and his two friends had been seized so lawlessly by the Linquan County thugs right outside the Petitions and Appeals Office. The county cadres must have slandered them for the Beijing comrades to stand by and see them taken away—the Beijing comrades must have been lied to. Thinking thus, Wang Hongchao decided that he must go again to Beijing to clarify the slanders heaped on him and the other village representatives. Wang Hongchao decided to act.

He remembered the "evidence" against him that had been read at the kangaroo trial. He started by looking up three people in the village who had supplied the court with evidence against him. What he heard gave Wang the shock of his life.

The first witness he looked up, a woman named Shao, had never showed up in court. When told that her evidence had been read out in court, she in turn got the shock of her life. She said that on the fateful night of April 2, she had gone to bed early and did not hear anything that happened in the village. Besides, she said, she was illiterate and had never given any evidence, much less made a mark with her thumb on any written document. "Either someone is out to hurt me," she said, "or someone is using me to hurt somebody else."

The second witness, also surnamed Wang, said that officers from the county security office had come visiting. They took out a photocopy and asked him to read it. He was illiterate, so the officers read out a list of names from the page and asked him, "Are these people from your village?" He said yes. Then the security officer took out another sheet of paper and started writing; when finished, he asked Wang to put his mark on the page. Wang of course didn't want to do anything of the sort. Then Baimiao Township Party Boss Han Chunsheng walked over and said, "Just make a mark with your thumb and get it over with." So Wang did as he was told and made a mark with his thumb first on the photocopied page and then on the written page. Only when the pages were read out in court did he realize that he had been made to give "evidence" to the "crimes" of Wang Hongchao and Wang Xiangdong.

The third witness stated that he never said anything about the accused "attacking the public security men." He told Wang Hongchao, "They made me talk, and they took notes, then they asked me to put down my mark, but they never read back to me what they had written. When they read out my 'evidence' in court, it was nothing like what I had said."

Two other men who were accused of attacking the police the night of April 2 also claimed that they had been framed, as they were not even at home at the time. One had been in Henan and the other in Shanxi Province.

Wang Hongchao was stunned by the revelations. Once again, near the end of 1994, Wang Hongchao gathered together a group of seventy-three villagers and they undertook a fourth march to Beijing to seek justice. This time the emphasis of the accusation was less on the unfair financial burdens as on the oppression that people suffered under County Party boss Zhang Xide.

When Zhang Xide heard that the Wang villagers were once again on the road to Beijing, he hit the roof. "I am going to get them," he said gnashing his teeth, "even if it costs me an arm and a leg."

The peasants' repeated trips to Beijing in the face of unremitting official harassment sent danger signals to officials all the way up to the provincial level. The Anhui authorities commissioned a joint investigation group made up of officials on the provincial, the prefectural, and the county levels. They set up shop in both Baimiao Township and Wang Village. But the joint investigation was a great disappointment—how could it be otherwise, seeing as how the county people were in effect investigating themselves!

We later had a chance to examine the formal report of the investigation. It totally avoided the subject of whether the peasants of Wang village had been overburdened, and its pages were littered with figures showing that the books were in good order and that there were no financial irregularities among the cadres of the village. Worse, the joint investigation's report concerning the "Baimiao Township incident" repeated the county authorities' allegations that Wang Junbin, Wang Xiangdong, Wang Hongchao, Wang Hongzhang and others were "criminals." As to the illegal secret detainment of Wang Hongchao, Wang Xiangdong, and Wang Hongqin in the Taihe County jail, the report falsely stated that the accused had all signed statements confessing to their crimes. Shielded by his superiors, Zhang Xide continued to lord it over the village unrestrained, becoming richer and richer in the process, even driving around in a Mercedes Benz, paid for by public money, of course.

Life dragged on through 1994 into 1995, when the peasants of Wang Village were afflicted with another punitive disaster. On September 1, 1995, Linquan County sent down another "shock team," this time with three hundred members, to check on the implementation of the one-child policy. These low-life creatures swaggered about the village, invented excuses to impose fines and taxes, and dragged away your pig or your sheep, dug up your grain storage, removed your furniture, broke down your door or wrecked the walls of your house in pursuit of fines and payments that would go into their own pockets. Again, the peasants were made to bear the burden of the shock team's expenses.

The residents of Wang Village were outraged. Yet again they held a meeting and yet again they decided to launch a march to Beijing to seek justice, their fifth march. There was no turning back, and they did not care to leave any room for maneuvering.

It was do or die. Leading this march was none other than the well-tested village representative, the former peddler of rat poison Wang Hongchao.

The group's arrival in Beijing did not take place in a vacuum. To the contrary, the atmosphere was already changed. Just a few weeks before, Li Xinwen, a peasant from another village of Linquan County had come to Beijing to petition for justice. Li's house had been forcibly demolished so that the county security bureau could build a fancy new office building on the site. Li had received no suitable compensation and in addition had been deprived of his livelihood. Now homeless, Li came to Beijing to look for justice, but was robbed of his money in the big city. On October 4, 1995—right after the forty-sixth anniversary of the founding of the People's Republic—Li, in complete despair, tried to throw himself under a car at a busy downtown intersection in the Qianmen district, but he did not succeed. At dawn the next morning, October 5, he went to the top of the Petitions and Appeals Office building and leaped to his death.

The city was shocked. The scandal of such a tragedy born of a peasant's hopelessness was followed on October 27 by the arrival in the capital of the seventy-four villagers from a village in Linquan County. It was the fifth desperate attempt of peasants from Wang Village of Baimiao Township, Linquan County, Anhui Province to get the attention of the Party and the government. Two days later, on October 29, a Sunday, they found themselves in Tiananmen Square.

The five-star national flag fluttered at the center of the square, and families were relaxing and enjoying themselves in the vicinity. The peasants of Wang Village eluded Appeals Office staff, who were keeping an eye on them. They managed to congregate at the foot of the pole that bore the national flag;

by prearranged signal, all fell down on their knees in mute accusation. The peasants of Wang Village had come to Beijing to beg the Party to redress their grievances: they had decided to take this action at the risk of their lives. They knew the implications of such an act—the negative effect it could have on the country's image. Making the country look bad could be construed as trying to smear the Party in a public arena exposed to the view of foreign reporters. They could be arrested, jailed—even shot. But they could think of no other way to move the Beijing leaders, whose hearts seemed deaf to the cries of the people.

The peasants of Linquan County—one who had jumped to his death in despair, and seventy-four who had traveled across the county to fall down on their knees in Tiananmen Square—finally had the nation's attention, and the nation was shaken to its core. The Party Central Committee finally sat up and took notice. Orders were sent off to the provincial leaders of Anhui to come to the capital immediately. They were to attend an emergency meeting with representatives from the Ministry of Agriculture, the Ministry of Public Security, the High Procurator's Court, the Judicial High Court, the Disciplinary Committee of the Central Committee, the National Birth Planning Committee, and other concerned offices and institutions.

Wang Hongchao and two other peasants were invited to attend and put their case before the august gathering.

At the meeting, leaders from the Ministry of Agriculture confirmed the Party Central Committee's policy of relieving the peasants' burdens and ordered reimbursement for any excessive fines and taxes imposed on them. It was also made clear that peasants should not be punished for going to the upper tiers of leadership to lay out their grievances.

The Party Central's Disciplinary Committee and the government's law enforcement expressed their disapproval of the procrastination and delays that had exacerbated the tensions between the peasants and the leadership. They announced that disciplinary measures would be meted out wherever necessary, including punishment by law. The representative from the Ministry of Public Security also clarified the issues related to the so-called Baimiao Township incident of April 2, 1994, and the crackdown that followed—which was the tipping point that pushed the peasants over the edge. The peasants also got answers to their questions about policemen going on patrols in villages: One, the public security's patrolling was conducted only in densely populated urban areas. Two, it was against the law for public security personnel to refuse to show their IDs. Three, the villagers were justified in smashing the van of strangers who sniffed around the village under cover of night and refused to show their IDs. And, finally, Four, those who had been arrested in the crackdown must be immediately released.

So much for the so-called "Baimiao Township incident" of April 2, 1994, which started when Village Chief Gao robbed Wang Hongchao of his TV and bike for nonpayment of a 6 yuan tax, an act of bullying that spiraled out of control, sparked the villagers' five trips to Beijing, and ended with the public spectacle of seventy-four peasants kneeling in supplication to the Party in the heart of Beijing.

A month later, in November 1995, the Anhui provincial government fielded a new investigation team made up of twelve comrades from the provincial and the prefecture levels and sent it down to Baimiao Township and Wang Village to do on-the-spot investigation. After a stay of twenty days the team was able to confirm that there had been excessive taxation, excessive use of force in implementing the one-child policy, and excessive measures in dealing with the so-called "Baimiao Township incident" of April 2, 1994. A fair summary. Sort of.

* * *

December 6, 1995, was a happy day in Wang Village.

Wang Xiangdong, one of the handful of young local men with some education and one of the three young men who had led the first expedition to Beijing in the winter of 1993, was released from prison after being illegally detained for one and a half years. After the crackdown following the Baimiao Township incident of April 2, 1994, he joined in leading the second trip to Beijing, together with Wang Hongchao and Wang Hongqin, then was dragged back from Beijing, thrown into jail in Taihe County, and later secretly sentenced to two years in prison.

Wang Junbin, the army veteran who had been on the wanted list, had gone into hiding after taking part in the first trip to Beijing. He led the third, unsuccessful, trip to Beijing in company with the newcomer on the scene, Wang Hongling; he was also the man whose brother had been wrongfully arrested for sending that mysterious telegram. He had been in hiding ever since. Now both returned triumphantly, and Wang Junbin was reinstated in the Party.

Wang Hongchao, the rat poison peddler, had taken an active role throughout the fight for justice. In addition to leading the first and second trips, after which he had been dragged back and thrown into jail, he led the fourth expedition, of seventy-three people, to Beijing. That expedition led to a joint investigation team, but it included the accused themselves—the county leadership—and thus came to nothing. Wang Hongchao was also the mind behind the fifth and last expedition to Beijing, when seventy-four peasants of Wang Village finally got the attention of the Party and the government.

Now all these men—Wang Junbin, Wang Hongchao, Wang Xiangdong, Wang Hongqin and others—were welcomed back like heroes, with a great banging of gongs and setting off of firecrackers and waving of red flags bearing accolades such as "Champions of the People."

Wang Xiangdong was elected the new village chief, and Wang Junbin was Party secretary.

The beginning of the year 1996 brought a thrill throughout the village community: Linquan County Party Boss Zhang Xide was being transferred! The news spread like wildfire. On the day that he was to leave, hundreds if not thousands from all the surrounding villages poured into the county seat and massed directly in front of the county Party headquarters, laying siege to Zhang Xide in his office. People shouted unceremoniously, "Zhang, come out and show your face!" County officials were among the spectators, but none stepped forward to defuse the situation.

Zhang Xide finally appeared shamefacedly. As he tried to express some words of apology, the crowd surged toward him, swept him up and pushed him down and tossed him about, some cursing, others surreptitiously using their fists. The once-formidable Party secretary of Linquan County flailed his hands about helplessly. How the mighty are fallen. The county public security force came to his rescue, their arrival preceded by the wail of police sirens, but the once-all-powerful Zhang Xide beseeched them, "Please, please don't make arrests! Please, don't hurt anybody!" It seemed that Zhang Xide had finally learned a lesson.

5

A VICIOUS CIRCLE

A Vicious Circle

Among the incidents of abuse in rural Anhui, one of the most shocking was the tragedy in Shensai Village, a typical case of tax extortion leading to a peasant's losing his life.

The village of Shensai, part of Zhonggang Township, Funan County, on the banks of the Huai River, is known far and wide as a "reservoir," in effect a spillway for the river. Whenever the Huai overflows its banks, the villagers have to see their fields become vast reservoirs to accommodate the rising waters and see their own homes float away with the flood. Year after year, they make this extreme sacrifice so that downstream, the city of Bengbu, the coal mines on the lower reaches of the river, the great city of Shanghai, and the bordering rich provinces of Jiangsu and Zhejiang can be spared. Year after year, the villagers must resign themselves to seeing everything that they have worked for inundated. People we talked to said that Heaven would punish anyone who dares take advantage of these long-suffering peasants. But the Party boss of Shensai Village, Shen Keli, was just such a man.

At one time Shen Keli had been a hearty young fellow. He signed up for the army and joined the Party soon after. When he was demobilized, the villagers felt that he had the right stuff and elected him chief of the villagers' committee. At the beginning he did indeed exert himself on behalf of his fellow villagers and he won their esteem. Soon he became Party boss as well as village chief and was even elected a delegate to the Township People's Congress.* As he rose in status, Shen began to see more of the world. He realized that public institutions big and small, which were supposed to be "serving the people," actually were being exploited and their powers used to extract what could be wrung from the people in the form of taxes, fines, fees, charges, and obligatory "fund-raising" for this or that cause. In a word, "serving the people" had become "serving the money god." Shen Keli got the picture and began to act on it. Through embezzlement, bribes, and extortion, Shen clawed his way to money and power. Next he turned his attention to the military. He appointed two of his three younger brothers to the militia: Shen Kexin, the eldest, became captain and Shen Kehui became a full-time member, and he equipped them with firearms and electric prods. He then appointed his youngest brother, Shen Chaoqun, as head of one of the production brigades in the village.** With this, Shen Keli had control of the Party, the civil administration, and the military, and became the absolute ruler of Shensai Village.

It was against this background that the infamous incident of armed extortion of the "village cash reserve" in Shensai Village took place on November 4, 1995, which led to two deaths, and a third man wounded. The incident caught the attention of the

* China's top legislative body is the National People's Congress. It makes the laws, and local people's congresses and governments produce local legislation.

**Administrative and production units in China have varied over time and also by locality. In the post-Liberation era the countryside was divided into communes, production brigades, and production teams. Nowadays village committees are more common.

Central Committee and the State Council. *Focus*, a popular program on China Central Television, broadcast an account of the incident, and this elicited calls for harsh punishments for the perpetrators and inquiries into the responsibility of leaders at higher levels involved in the case. Both Shen Keli and his brother, Shen Kexin, were stripped of their political rights for life. Moreover, Militia Captain Shen Kexin, the principal perpetrator in the incident, was sentenced to death for premeditated murder, and Village Chief Shen Keli received the death sentence, with probation. Just as the provincial high court confirmed the sentences and ordered the immediate execution of Shen Kexin, a new order came from Beijing to delay the execution until CCTV readied itself for live broadcast, obviously to send a message to the nation at large. This was totally unprecedented in the history of the nation.

The sentencing and subsequent decision to televise the execution had some interesting fallout, for it created a predicament for the local government. It had been decided that the formal announcement of the death sentence and the execution to follow would take place in the county seat instead of the more usual location, the provincial capital. The county leadership became uneasy at the possible movements of Beijing TV reporters in their locality: housed in the county area, they might quite possibly nose around in Shen Village and see the abject poverty everywhere. So the reporters were put up in the county's best hotel with young female attendants to keep them happy. Even so, the reporters still managed to steal into Shensai Village and make video recordings of what they saw.

On the eventful day when thousands if not millions witnessed Shen Kexin being led off to the execution ground, live on TV, announcements were made on *Focus* of disciplinary measures and administrative demotions to be meted out to leaders at prefecture, county, and township levels. The broadcast ended with words quoted from Zhu Rongji, then premier of the State Council: "From this day on, anybody who ignores rules and squeezes the peasants will have to answer for himself!"

The Party Central Committee and the State Council also jointly issued a document regarding the Shensai incident that called national attention to the problem of excessive taxation of the peasants. "Briefing on Serious Incidents in 1995 Relating to Overtaxation of the Peasants" revealed that in 1995 alone there had been thirteen cases in eight provinces of excessive taxation leading to loss of life among the peasantry. The case of Shensai Village in Anhui Province was only one of many, and it was used to make an example and send a strong signal.

The joint document traveled down through the tiers of government to the village level, so that all and sundry were put on notice that excessive burdens would not be tolerated, but it was not enough to prevent the tragedy of Zhang Village (see chapter 2, "The Village Tyrant"), in which four peasants were killed and one wounded. After the Zhang Village incident, eight similar cases were reported in 1999—three in Hunan, two in Sichuan, and one case each in the provinces of Hubei, Gansu, and Henan. Who knows the number of cases that went unreported? Many of our countrymen in rural areas have lost their lives trying to resist excessive taxes. Meanwhile the Party and the government have issued one directive after another, laying down rules and prohibitions, but taxes keep being piled on the peasant population.

When we examine the wording of those authoritative documents, we notice that many of them were limited to laying down principles, or "spirit." Practice could not be checked against these principles, nor did the prohibitions carry legal weight. Consequently, what was to be abolished continued to flourish; what was to be changed remained business as usual; what was to be halted continued unchecked. The excessive taxation targeted by the Party's and State Council's rules and restrictions became like the chives in the popular proverb: "The more you lop them off the faster they grow." It seems that the problem of the peasants' excessive taxes has evolved into a vicious circle: the more directives prohibiting taxation, the more taxation there is.

In our own investigations in fifty of so counties in the province of Anhui, we did not find one single county that did not cut corners in implementing those directives—that is, if they did so at all. This situation is hardly likely to be limited to Anhui.

Li Changping, the Party boss of Jianli County, Hubei Province, who had made a name for himself a few years earlier by writing bluntly of the peasants' plight to the Central Committee, summed up the current situation: "The Party Central Committee knows perfectly well that although problems appear at the bottom, the root lies with the top leadership. Why not pursue it at the top? If the leadership refuses to dig up the root of the problems, local officials will only be more emboldened, the bureaucratic machine will continue to grow, while the peasants' burden will be heavier and heavier. In which case the policies of the Party would be like 'ears for the deaf' in the popular saying: just put up for show."

In 1994, when the peasants were already feeling the pinch, the government decided to introduce a tax reform whereby state and local taxes would be separated into two parallel systems and taxation would thus be decentralized. When the central government had supreme control of tax monies, local governments faced a budgetary crisis. Income tends to flow up, to the central government, while expenses get passed down, to the local government. Spending on basic public services such as education, family planning, veteran's pensions and so on were all relegated to the local level. The state's new policy with regard to local income was: "no tax on surplus; no subsidy for deficit; more income, more spending." Yet this policy had the effect of encouraging officials at county and township levels to squeeze the rural economy and exploit the peasants in order to run their own bureaucracies. The peasants' burden began to spiral out of control.

According to statistics released by the state for the year 1995, taxation on rural products increased by 19.9 percent over the previous year; payment of local "reserve funds" for various causes grew by 48.3 percent; and the payment of fines, fees, charges, and contributions to public projects grew by 52.22 percent. The tax burden of one third of the peasant population nationwide far exceeded 5 percent of their annual income from the previous year—the designated limit for taxation of peasant households. The popular saying goes: "So many hands left and right, all stretched out for the peasant's mite."

In 1996, the Central Committee and State Council issued another joint document, titled "Decision Regarding the Relief of Peasants' Burdens," which was widely publicized as the "Number 13 Circular." The "Number 13 Circular" announced disciplinary measures to be taken against officials at various levels in cases of major incidents of tax extortion resulting in death; of retaliation against peasants for making complaints; of failure to report incidents arising out of excessive taxation; or of minimizing damage in such reports. The Party requested that the "Number 13 Circular" be made known to every tier of the government and publicized to every peasant household. It also called for legislation for supervising the measures taken to relieve the peasants' burden. To ensure that the "Number 13 Circular" was observed, a central joint inspection team made up of personnel from the various ministries and the media was sent out to the provinces of Henan, Hunan, Hubei, Anhui, and Shanxi to ensure that the "Number 13 Circular" was duly publicized and the relief policies implemented. These were unprecedented measures to enforce Party policy—yet precisely during this period the peasants' tax burden broke the record. According to official statistics, from 1991 to 1993, income from agricultural taxes was only 2.2 percent of the national tax income, but in 1996—the year the "Number 13 Circular" was issued and implemented—the percentage jumped to 5.3 percent, more than double the figure for the previous years.

Figures for 1997 were no better. The price of agricultural products fell steeply in Anhui as for the whole country, and so did the rate of growth in peasant income. Increases in productivity did not bring comparable increases in earnings, but the fees, charges, and taxes levied by local governments continued to grow. According to official statistics, peasants' average yearly income from 1994 to 1997 was only 1.91 percent more than it had been in 1993—but the tax burden for 1997 was nine times the average of the previous four years.

To look at the problem from another angle: during the early years of reform, at the beginning of the eighties, the cost for planting one *mu* (approximately one and a half acres) of land was 10 yuan, and peasants paid their taxes automatically, without any prodding from local cadres. Nowadays, however, the cost for planting the same piece of land was at least one hundred yuan, in some cases running to two to three hundred. The resulting taxes and fees obviously exceeded the peasants' ability to pay. To deal with the problem, local administrations would send out "shock teams" of tax collectors to enforce payment. When the peasants could not come up with the cash, the shock teams would take away their pigs, or make off with a piece of furniture or machinery. When this still didn't work, violence was the answer: beatings, arrests, detention, and other dictatorial measures. Hostility between peasants and administration was acute; peasants' appeals, petitions, and demonstrations became the order of the day. It was just such a situation that touched off the mass arrests in Gao Village, when a convoy of armed police and officials descended on a group of totally unarmed peasants during a noon break (see chapter 3, "The Long and the Short of the Antitax Uprising").

By 1998, the situation was so bad that the Central Committee and the State Council felt obliged to send out another directive, instructing officials at all levels to take seriously the letters of complaints and personal appeals coming from peasants. They were cautioned to listen to the voice of the masses, nip any potential problems in the bud, and limit unrest to local levels. In spite of these repeated orders and directives, six violent incidents similar to the Zhang Village tragedy erupted simultaneously in six different provinces in that same year.

"It's Fine to Have a Policy, But Who Will Carry It Out?"

China's reform was first tried out in rural Anhui, and many top people emerged through that great experiment—people who were familiar with rural conditions, cared for the peasants, and were not afraid to speak their minds.

Lu Zixiu was such a person. During the late seventies, he distinguished himself by promoting so-called "household contracts," one of the important aspects of the economic reform being tried out in rural Anhui.* When we met him on a June day in 2001, he had already retired from his position as deputy chair of the Anhui People's Congress, but had never stopped concerning himself with rural issues.

* Under the "household-contract responsibility system," each household was given a piece of land to farm and was allowed to retain whatever was left after selling to the state a fixed proportion of what they had produced, at state-determined prices, or by simply paying a tax in cash.

Lu described for us a meeting that he had once attended. The Anhui provincial leadership had called the meeting of provincial and prefectural Party leaders, and the topic of the day was an overview of how the Central Committee's directives about relieving the peasants' burden had been implemented throughout the province. At the meeting, some of the attendees started to air their own tales of woe, the difficulties they were encountering in their domains. Lu did not like what he was hearing; he was very familiar with these municipal and prefecture leaders and had no scruples about giving them a tongue lashing.

Since the meeting was held in Fuyang Prefecture, Lu Zixiu started with the Party secretary of the prefecture. Calling him unceremoniously by name,* he launched his interrogation aggressively: "You there, Wang Huaizhong, you answer only to your provincial superiors sitting over there, hey? You don't answer to the peasants? You don't give a damn how they can manage to support your fancy projects? You set yourself up to create a 'dairy' county, but all your 'dairy farms' are lined along the highways for show! At one of your 'on-site' meetings, you rent cows at great expense to make an impression! Is this how you spend the peasants' hard-earned pennies?"

Before the man could respond, Lu turned to the party secretary of Chuzhou Prefecture: "And you, Zhang Chunsheng, how do you handle your subordinates? Tell us, how do you evaluate performances? Those bullies who extort payments and force peasants into committing suicide, you just move them to another cushy spot, hey, so long as they can come up with the dough!"

Next he asked the Party secretary of Bengbu: "And you, Fang Yiben, Huaiyuan County is under your jurisdiction. Accusations and complaints are piling up by the day . . . Have

* Failing to use the Party secretary's title—"calling unceremoniously by name"—implies an inappropriate familiarity, an intended show of disrespect.

you done anything about it? Are you trying to win the championship for highest volume of peasants' complaints?

Then he pointed a finger at the Party secretary of Chaohu Prefecture: "You, Hu Jiduo, do you mean to say that you can't pave a highway without screwing the peasants? That highway should be paid for by the state! But you don't give a damn for the highway. You are paving credit for yourself, for the eyes of your bosses! Am I right?"

According to Lu's account to us, he made a round of all of the officials at the meeting and ended by saying: "I'd like to address this to our comrades: we see the high-rises, but do we care who built them? We see the highways, but do we know who paved them? Right now with the reform, the peasants are just beginning to see a turnaround in their lives. But we can't wait to pounce on them to empty their pockets! Give them a break, for heaven's sake!" He recalled the early years of rural reform: "During the 'household-contract' movement, the working principle was 'pay the state in full, reserve what is necessary for the collective, and the rest is yours to keep.' And it worked! Now, however, all the advantages of the contract system are slipping away, quietly stolen from the peasants by government taxes at every level. The peasants have no rights at all. You can do whatever you like with them. Why don't we try to look at things from the peasants' point of view?"

The Party secretary of Liu-An Prefecture put in a word: "At least we don't have a problem with excessive taxes—" Before the words were out of his mouth, Lu Zixiu cut him short: "Don't talk to me about your taxes—I have a bunch of letters on my desk! Your peasants have barely planted a tree in the ground before your local cadres knock on their doors for taxes on the produce!" The complacent Party secretary was effectively shut up.

During a break, the provincial Party secretary, who was

chairing the meeting, came up to Lu Zixiu and said to him privately, "Well done, well done—"

"Well done my ass," Lu retorted. "Why don't you say that openly? I am your hit man, I do it with my eyes open, and that's that!"

Thus Lu Zixiu's graphic description of that meeting not only created a sketch of the prevailing problems in rural China but at the same time revealed his own temperament.

A story about Lu Zixiu that we heard from other sources serves as a good illustration of the man and his style. At one point in his career, Lu had been Party secretary for Chuzhou Prefecture. One day the director of the General Office of the Central Committee, Wen Jiabao, arrived on an inspection tour. Lu Zixiu greeted his superior with the question "What do you want to see, director, the true or the false? The situation as it really is, or the flashy stuff?" Director Wen smiled and said, "Let's take a look at both!" Years later, in 1996, at a national conference on rural poverty relief, Wen Jiabao,* who was chairing the meeting, spotted Lu Zixiu among the delegates and beckoned to him. "Tell me, what is the critical issue in agriculture?" Lu Zixiu went right to the point: "Cadres. It's fine to have a policy, but who will carry it out?"

Our interview with Lu Zixiu went very well. When we mentioned that we were doing a comprehensive study of the peasant problem, he opened up further. "In the past," he said, "Mao Zedong said that 'a serious problem is educating the peasants.' I would rather say that the serious problem today is ensuring

*The current (2005) premier of China.

the interests of the peasants. If the peasants' interests are overlooked, agricultural growth, social development, and political stability are just empty words." He went on to quote Lenin: "Lenin warned that 'capitalism is cropping up among us every moment, every day.' But what's wrong with that? Isn't it better than feudalism cropping up among us every moment, every day?"

Lu summed up his views by quoting Emperor Taizong of the Tang Dynasty. "Over a thousand years ago, Emperor Taizong said, 'Water holds up the boat; water can also sink the boat.' Water here refers to the peasants. Emperor Taizong realized the importance of the peasantry. Each and every dynasty understood full well the importance of the peasantry, but once they are in power, they turn around and exploit the peasantry, even suppress the peasantry. Using history as a mirror, the Chinese Communist Party is faced with the same problem."

Brief History of the Chinese Peasants' Burden

China is a vast agricultural country with over three thousand years of recorded history, and peasants make up the overwhelming majority of the population. Thus it is inevitable that the problem of the peasants' burden surfaces again and again in every dynasty, and will not go away.

In the early years of the People's Republic of China, the central government was preoccupied with dealing with inflation and unemployment and preparing for the country's industrialization. It could not concern itself with budgetary problems in the vast rural areas, and did not interfere when local governments took things into their own hands and imposed supplementary taxes over the regular agricultural taxes. There was a limit imposed on these supplementary taxes, of course, but when the local administration was short of cash, there was nothing to stop them from inventing new excuses to squeeze the peasants.

The Korean War in 1951 followed the tension of the early period, with economic sanctions imposed on China by Western countries. In face of the situation at home and abroad, the Party and central government had no choice but to prioritize industrialization and accumulate capital at the cost of agricultural development.

Over a period of thirty long years, the peasants of China carried this heavy burden. But the burden was hidden, because the state ceased to deal directly with individual peasants. The 130 million peasant households soon metamorphosed into 7 million mutual-help groups, and then into 790,000 agricultural cooperatives. The whirlwind of the Great Leap Forward in 1958 took barely three months to convert these cooperatives into 52,781 people's communes, to the fanfare of drum beating and cymbal banging; not a single peasant eluded the net.

It is impossible to do justice to the magnitude of the sacrifice that the peasants made toward the accumulation of capital for China's industrialization. It is safe to say that the edifice of China's industry is built from the flesh and blood of toiling peasants, and urban development was achieved through their pain and sacrifice.

Beginning in the early 1950s, collectivization was forcibly promoted through political and administrative measures in the absence of consultation regarding the wishes of the peasants. From then on, agriculture—what to plant and what to grow—was done according to orders from above. In 1956, the year of collectivization, agriculture visibly declined; this was obvious even before the harvest was taken in. Many peasants simply wanted out. Resistance was widespread, sometimes ending up in mass protests or petitions to Beijing. In some cases, peasants went so far as to break up the cooperatives on their own initiative and distribute the collectively owned land and grain. The resistance to collectivization and its re-enforcement entailed violence on both sides. Peasants besieged leading officials in county centers, or ransacked security offices. Local cadres for their part labeled the peasants' actions attacks on the Party and on socialism, labels which would legitimize the use of force against the peasants. Beatings and struggle sessions led to death for some, forced suicide for others. By 1957, the terror of the "antirightist" movement—in which half a million people who had answered Mao's call to "bloom and contend" by expressing their opinions were then labeled "rightists" and mercilessly persecuted—effectively wiped out the last remnants of the peasants' resistance to collectivization.

The Great Leap Forward in 1958 swept through the countryside like a whirlwind, plucking the peasants from the cooperatives, still shaky from the recent turmoil, and marshaling them into even bigger collective units, called people's communes. Now, any property that the peasants owned or had acquired through land reform—land, animals, implements, grain, even personal belongings—were taken away without compensation. The formation of more than fifty thousand people's communes was tantamount to the state's opening fifty thousand new accounts in rural areas on which it could draw at will: all the finances and labor power and other resources of the communes were at the disposal of the state.

The peasants of China had truly become the proletariat, owning nothing but their chains!

Following on the heels of the people's communes was the "instant entry into communism" experiment, which was tried out in many designated rural areas. In order to abolish private property so as to enter "communism," peasants had to give up household property such as cupboards or trunks for clothes to the commune. Cooking utensils were smashed and hurled into furnaces for making steel, to fulfill the steel production target of the Great Leap Forward. The peasants were hit hard; understandably, they lost all incentive to work. Work slowdowns spread through rural China like a plague, and agricultural production declined sharply.

Records show that in the year after the creation of the communes in 1958, agricultural production dropped by 13.4 percent, but the state's conscription of grain increased by 14.7 percent for the same period. Agricultural production dropped a further 15.6 percent in 1960; nationwide only 287 billion *jin* (1 *jin* is slightly over a pound) of grain were produced. But the state's conscription of grain for that year was still increased. In some cases, seeds and the family's food grain had to be given up to the cities or for export, to fill the state's demands. In order for production figures to "leap forward," local cadres had no choice but to resort to inflating their figures for the eyes of their superiors. Take for instance the case of Feixi County. Feixi was a middle-sized agricultural county, but it reported a harvest of 400 million *jin* of grain production, more than double the true figure. How are the peasants to survive if conscription of grain is based on inflated figures like these? The answer was obvious— by now, the peasants' problem was not excessive taxes but death by starvation. It is impossible to imagine how many peasants' lives were sacrificed on the altar of the commune. It is said that in Fengyang County alone the death toll was 60,245—17.7 percent of the county's population. Two hundred and forty complete households starved to death. Twenty-seven villages disappeared altogether from the county map, wiped out by death and migration. In Xia Huang Village of Damiao Commune, one of the worst-hit communes in the county, the death toll was 68.6 percent of the population.

It is not surprising that years later, during the Cultural

Revolution, when many peasants were made to recite their sufferings in the "old" society and sing the blessings of the "new," their memories of misfortune derived not from pre-Liberation days, but from the starvation of the 1960s, the most tragic event in their living memory. And yet our official version of history defines this monstrous tragedy as the result of "three years of natural disasters."

After the "natural disasters" of the early 1960s came the ten years of the Cultural Revolution (1966–1976), when an ultra-leftist critique of capitalism was pushed to monstrous extremes. A peasant would be accused of "taking the capitalist road" if his household kept two chickens or planted a few vegetables for the market. Agriculture was so devastated that by the end of the Cultural Revolution, figures released for 1977 show that the value of one day's labor in the people's commune averaged 11 cents, barely enough to buy one pack of the cheapest cigarettes in the rural market. To put it another way, in Anhui as well as in some other provinces, a peasant's average day's work could not produce as much grain as that of his or her Han Dynasty counterpart two thousand years ago!

When the Cultural Revolution was finally brought to a halt, following Mao's death in 1976, the household-contract system was tried out in Anhui Province and proved a great success. The lethargy of the previous years was gone. One would frequently see three generations of a family working together under one of these contracts, looking toward a better life. This reform saw a sustained 15 percent increase of per capita income for the years 1978 to 1984. It was the years of recovery. The long-standing policy prohibiting the free sale of grain and other agricultural products was eased. The government's monopoly of grain purchases at fixed prices, which had been in place for four decades, was gradually abolished.

* * *

But just as the restrictions were easing, the Third Plenary Session of the Twelfth National Party Congress convened in December of 1984, a great historical turning point.* The Twelfth Party Congress announced the launch of comprehensive reform in urban areas. Thus, the focus of China's ongoing reform efforts would shift from rural to urban, and so would capital investment. Once again, the burden of this massive project fell on the shoulders of the peasants.

In order to simplify the administrative process of securing income from rural taxation, the government converted the discredited people's communes into over sixty thousand administrative townships and invested them with power to impose and collect taxes.

Once established, inevitably this lowest rung of state bureaucracy began to expand. Just as in the traditional Chinese saying: "Tiny the sparrow may be, no part is missing that one can see," so the township administration was equipped with the six divisions of their counterparts in the upper echelons of power: Party, government, Party Disciplinary Committee, People's Congress, People's Consultative Conference, and the armed forces. Later added to this were the likewise analogous so-called "seven offices and eight stations": finance, taxation, public security, trade and industry, transportation, public health, grain control, agricultural technology, irrigation, seed control, soil erosion control, agricultural machinery, veterinary service, food control, fisheries, and so on. Thus the scale of the township bureaucracy continued to grow.

The cost of maintaining this burgeoning bureaucracy was of course left to the peasants, always at the bottom of the complex. The peasants' burden, previously hidden within the mech-

---

* The National Party Congress is in theory the highest body of the Communist Party of China (to be distinguished from the National People's Congress). For further information, see "National Party Congresses," http://countrystudies.us/china/101.htm.

anism of the people's communes, now emerged into the open in the form of taxes.

Following on this administrative "reform," which left peasants to the tender mercies of township officials, the central government introduced new rules regarding rural taxation for community welfare, village officials' salaries, village administration, primary and secondary education, family planning, veterans' benefits, militia training, road works, and other public service. Those services, which should be supported by the state, were now deposited on the backs of the peasants, who had no say in the matter.

Under the relentless demands for money to cover administrative expenses, fund-raising projects, fines, fees, and allocated contributions, the peasants lost their enthusiasm for reform that had characterized the early days. Wan Li, chair of the Standing Committee of the National People's Congress, a man who had distinguished himself in pushing for rural reform, said at a meeting in the late eighties: "The peasants' gains must not be taken back. We must issue another document to encourage the peasants to move onward. Otherwise, the peasants will cease to listen to the Party." Despite Wan Li's admonishments, however, the peasants' meager gains through the early years of the reform were being eroded.

In 1978, the decision at the third plenary session of the Eleventh Party Congress had established the target that 18 percent of the state's total investment in the economy should be in agriculture. But this figure was never realized. The slogan was repeated from year to year, but in practice, the state left the growth of investment in agriculture to the peasants themselves.

With the reform's shift of emphasis from the rural to the urban economy, the disparity between city and country continued to grow: urban development grew by leaps and bounds and people's living standards continued to rise, while the rural areas remained stagnant and lagged further behind. Between 1989 and 1991, when there were strong harvests and growth was in the double digits, the peasants' per capita income grew only 2 percent per annum on average, though there was no growth for the year 1991. A second phase of slowdown in income growth occurred after 1996, when the rate of increase in peasants' per capita income dropped for two straight years, from 9 percent to 4.0 percent growth in 1998.

In ten years, between 1990 and 2000, the total of all the taxes that the state had extracted from the peasants had increased by a factor of five, from over 8.7 billion yuan to over 46.5 billion yuan. By 2000, the peasants' tax burden averaged 146 yuan per head, six times the average urban resident's tax burden of merely 37 yuan per head. Yet city dwellers' income was on average six times the peasants' income! This in itself is already a grave injustice, but over and above regular taxation, the peasants had to suffer further extortion for village reserves and fees for social services.

How Do I Tax Thee? Let Me Count the Ways.

As we made our way through fifty or so counties over a two-year period, we tried to get an answer to the question: How much are peasants taxed? Surprisingly, no one had an authoritative answer. So all we could do was make a list of what we were able to put together from asking around.

According to the statistics of the government's Department for Supervising the Peasants' Burdens, there are ninety-three categories of fees and charges, funds and reserves, devised by the State Council and the various ministries whose activities involve the rural economy.

The various tiers of local governments list a total of 269 types of tax, but this figure does not include the payments that lower levels of administration tag on to government taxes, literally called "hitching a free ride."

And then there are the local inventions, which often come across like inspired black humor, but that does not affect the deadly seriousness with which payments are extracted. Absurd they may be; nevertheless they must be paid down to every last penny.

Among the devious rural tax schemes are the following:

"fund-raising"
Building the township office building
Building the township school
Setting up the township technology website,
Building the township outpatient clinic
Building the township broadcasting station
Building the township movie theater
Promoting township enterprise
Improving the township environment and striking
     down crime

Management Fees
Repairing village office quarters
Village cadres' allowance for business trips and
     entertainment
Activities of the village Party and Communist Youth League
Township Party Congress and People's Congress

Stipends for Village's Nonproduction Personnel
Party secretary
Village chief (chairman of village committee)
Chairwoman of village women's committee
Village group leaders

Captain of village militia
Member of village committee for security
Secretary of the village Communist Youth League
Vet
Broadcaster
Agricultural technician
Forest guard
Guard of sliding slopes
Newspaper delivery man
Street cleaner
Electrician
Plumber
Carpenter
Mason

Education expenses
Salary of village school teachers
Stipend for teachers in public schools
School building repair
Office expenses
Purchase of books, newspapers, and other materials
Purchase of teaching equipment
Purchase of sports equipment

Village birth-control project
Stipend for the single-child family
Nutrition allowance for postabortion operations
Stipend for member of village committee for birth planning
Stipend for group leader of village birth-planning program

Militia Training
Living expenses during training
Stipend for loss of work hours during training
Stipend for safeguarding firearms and cartridges

Social Services
Building the village old people's home
Stipend for workers at said home
Group health plan
Stipend for village health workers
Preferential treatment for surviving members of revolutionary martyrs and retired army personnel
Preferential treatment for disabled veterans
Preferential treatment for family members of army personnel in active service
Preferential treatment for workers hurt in work-related accidents
Preferential treatment for families in hardship
Preferential treatment for the aged who have lost their families

Aside from these formally listed items, innumerable other payments are extracted from the peasants on the spur of the moment for such purposes as "building a civilized village," widening the street to open a market, planning a house site, getting permission to build a private home, inspecting seed, obtaining antivirus shots for domestic poultry, maintaining troughs for domestic animals, connecting electric cables, eliminating rats, purchase of walkie-talkies and motorcycles for the local police, ordering uniforms for local law enforcement officials . . . and so on.

For children in school, apart from regular tuition, there are enforced "donations" to support education, charges for tutoring, charges for the price of examination papers, charges for the purchase of study materials, charges for the purchase of a broom for classroom cleaning.

If you are so enterprising as to keep a pig, you will need to pay the "live pig" tax, the pig killing tax, the "capital gain" tax, the income tax, and the tax toward maintenance of the township. In some places, you are taxed for keeping a pig whether you keep one or not.

The most outrageous case of "fancy" taxation that we came across were the taxes and payments in a certain township for getting married. The happy couple has to pay for the cost of the marriage certificate—the paper it is printed on. Then there are fees for the letter of authorization (provided by the work unit or by the village committee, certifying identity and age of applicants); the notary; the prenuptial physical (presumably checking for infectious disease), and a fee for a comprehensive physical for the bride. After these preliminaries, there is a deposit for commitment to the one-child family, a deposit for commitment to family planning, and a deposit for commitment to deferred pregnancy. After the birth-control part is taken care of, there is a deposit for commitment to "mutual devotion," and a deposit for a "golden wedding." Apart from these deposits, there is a tax for the wedding banquet, a tax for pig killing, a "green" tax for banquet-related environmental hazards, and finally a donation to the "Happy Children's Center."

The best example of finding excuses to impose new taxes would be the tax on cooking. Since the government's promulgation of the national "Environmental Protection Law," officials in some areas have invented the "hazardous waste disposal tax," slapped on peasant households on account of the family cooking.

And finally, there is a tax to ensure that all taxes are promptly paid, and that is the "attitude tax." If you dare to challenge or resist the tax collector who comes knocking at your door, you are capped with a "bad attitude" label, and that entails an extra tax.

* * *

The central government and its various institutions profit by prying taxes out of the peasants. The directives, orders, and regulations from the State Council are but pieces of paper handed down the various levels of government and read out—but that is all that happens: they are papers to be read. No matter how these orders are devised, there are always ways to work around them. Take, for instance, the government's policy on birth control. Once left in the hands of village cadres, the same sound policy could be downright barbarous in practice. One of the "precepts" that local cadres are guided by is: "Do not pluck from the water; do not snatch the bottle; do not cut down the rope." This murky rule means that it was more important for these village cadres to enforce the one-child policy than to save the lives of people who resisted the policy by threatening suicide by drowning, taking poison, or hanging themselves. In reality, these cadres discovered that the authority invested in them to implement the one-child policy turned into a veritable gold mine. It was discovered that in a single village in Suixi County, a birth-control inspection team had imposed more than three million yuan in fines during one month of "inspections." The team had replaced the enforcement of the one-child policy and the various "precepts" related to it with fines, thus opening the door to unlimited births so long as the families could pay the fines. As a result, unplanned births came to one hundred thousand for that county alone. (The vice chairman of the Anhui Provincial People's Congress gave us this information from the 1990s.)

We also came across a bizarre court case in Lixin County. Three cadres from Sunmiao Township—Yuan Zhidong, Li Peng, and Lin Ming—had run a clandestine "population education center" from December 1998 until their scam was uncovered in the summer of 1999. During this six-month period, equipped with vans and with hired thugs to do the dirty work, these three cadres had arrested and detained over two hundred people from twenty-two villages in the township, charged them with violating the one-child policy or obstruction of official business, or with no excuse at all, and put their victims under illegal detention. The unfortunate villagers were held in three rooms at a secret location; the windows were sealed and there was no lighting. People were forced to stay in the dark—eating, sleeping, relieving themselves within that same unbearably filthy, stinky area—not knowing whether it was day or night. Three older women, Mrs. Diao, Mrs. Wang, and Mrs. Xiao, were taken on the pretext that their daughters-in-law had missed the mandatory periodic check for pregnancy. A younger woman, Li Ying, had had complications during labor. She was rushed from the township to the county hospital for an operation, and was arrested for not giving birth at the "designated facility." Mrs. Qiu was arrested for getting pregnant right after the wedding instead of waiting for her turn according to the quota system,* while another young woman, Mrs. Luo, was taking care of her aunt's children and was arrested by mistake. The young Mrs. Zhou had gone to the township clinic for an abortion and was taken away by the three thugs for three days without an explanation. Most outrageous was the case of a young woman, Ma Yin, who had conceived without prior permission; while in detention she went into labor and had to give birth under appalling circumstances. When her father and younger sister rushed to the place of detention to help her, they were held hostage before she could be released with her newborn baby.

* Quotas for births were distributed according to a central plan, and couples had to wait for permission before starting to try for a baby. These quotas are no longer enforced.

All these illegal proceedings were undertaken with one end in mind: to extort money.

Ru Zipei of Shuangmiao Village had been working in the city for many years and was suspected of having made a small fortune. He became a main target and was one of the first to be detained; after eighteen grueling days in the dark room, he coughed up 8,000 yuan and was promptly released. A trio of young men all surnamed Zhou, who had also worked as migrants in the city, were taken together on the same day in early January. After five days in detention, the three jointly paid 10,000 yuan in cash and were set free. But an older man, Ma Yuerong, of Ruzhai Village had just had his home destroyed by fire and was unable to produce any cash. He was detained for one hundred and seventy days, and when he was finally released, he had started going deaf. Lixin County was designated a poor county by the state, and many villagers' lives were destroyed by the crushing fines. Some had to take loans, some had to sell their houses or whatever they owned and were left with nothing to live on.

The villagers were very disappointed at how lightly the three villains got off. Apart from running the illegal "population education center," these three rascals had given false witness, embezzled public funds, helped their superiors embezzle public funds, and committed many other offenses against the law. But the three got only light sentences of one year to three years, with probation. Their vile offenses had been committed right under the noses of the township leadership over a long period of time and had provoked a major public outcry when exposed, yet not a single local official took any responsibility for the disgraceful affair. People were very disillusioned.

The Village Anticorruption Bureau

Since they had no channel to air their grievances and often suffered retaliation if they did speak out, the long-suffering peasants sometimes resorted to other means of protest, occasionally showing great ingenuity.

This happened one day in Dongliu Village, Fengmiao Township, Lingbi County. The village Party boss, Shi Hua, took it into his head to collect some taxes. To ensure compliance, Shi got an official from the township administration to lend a hand, and also brought a bunch of thugs to do the dirty work.

Traveling by tractor, the group first went to Gao Village.

When Gao Chuanming couldn't come up with the cash, the gang just followed their usual procedure: ransack the family grain stores.

After dealing with Gao Chuanming's grain stores, the gang headed for the next target, but by then the whole village was alerted and came to the rescue of the intended victim. The two sides clashed and the villagers pushed the offending tractor into a pond nearby. The tractor's owner begged the villagers to spare his tractor—it had only been lent for the occasion, he explained, trying to distance himself from the tax-collecting gang. So the tractor was spared.

Seeing that the villagers were up in arms, the tax collectors decided to retreat. In their haste they stumbled into the home of Zhang Jidong. The pursuing group of villagers pursued them into Zhang's house, demanding an explanation. "Do you call yourself Communists?" "Do you have a conscience?" "How are we to live if this goes on?" Faced with the crowd, the tax collectors apologized right and left, saying that they were acting on orders. However, a few words of apology were not enough for the villagers, and the situation became tense. Then, one of the bullies backed down, promising that they would let their superiors at the township know the feelings of the people, and gradually the turmoil subsided.

Zhang Jidong, at one time an activist for villagers' rights, did not trust any promise made by this crowd. He knew them all too well. Having been humiliated, they were certain to seek retaliation later on. If not for the strong stand taken by the villagers, his own grain stores would have been ransacked that day. He felt sure that the villagers would have to pay dearly for their clash with the tax-collecting group. He gritted his teeth and took out a hundred-yuan note from his pocket, and stuffed it into the hand of the leader saying, "This is pitiful, I am so embarrassed. Just a trifle to get a few packs of cigarettes to calm down your men. Right now life is getting harder and harder and the villagers feel a lot of pent-up resentment. Hope you don't take it personally . . . "

Things turned out exactly as Zhang Jidong had feared. Not long afterward, the township military turned out in full force, led by the captain, Liu Huanchang. He put together a three-hundred-strong tax-enforcement team made up of stalwarts picked from ten villages within the township. At the head of the group were the uniformed township security personnel sporting police batons, with handcuffs jangling at their sides. They were followed by security guards from the various villages, decked out in camouflage. They proceeded to the villages as if they were penetrating enemy territory, faces set in stony determination, like some bad imitation of a squadron of commandos. Following on the heels of this formidable armed advance was an array of village chiefs riding on two tractors and seventeen motorized tricycles.

Where should they begin? The people of Wangyang Village were adamantly opposed to paying excess taxes and firmly united in their resistance, therefore it was decided that Wangyang Village was exactly where they should start. The villagers were scattered in the fields or working on the threshing ground, but they immediately fled back to the village when they got word of the coming invasion. The first thing the tax-enforcement team did was to seal off all the exits of the village. Then they occupied the village proper and the action started in earnest. They pounced on the grain stores of Lu Shuji, carting off 1,600 *jin* of grain. Next were the grain stores of two other villagers, Wang Ruxiu and Wang Shuwei; each was robbed of over 400 *jin* of grain. Then the tax collectors confiscated 200 yuan of Wang Shiming's, which the man had saved to buy fertilizer for his corn and cotton. During the process of confiscating grain and snatching cash, the tax collectors also hit and injured two villagers, Song and Cao.

By lucky, or unlucky, coincidence, a Taiwan businessman, Wang Yingqiu, who had been born in Wangyang Village, had sent his representative to make a study of the environment for possible investment in a manufacturing enterprise in his home village. The representative was caught in the middle of the tax-enforcement violence. He tried to take shots of the scene with his camera and got a few knocks himself. When the incident was reported to the Taiwan businessman, one can imagine the result. Thus ended the native son's hope of making some contribution toward the development of his home village.

Having suffered much at the hands of the invading tax-collecting squadron, Wangyang Village erupted like a volcano. The villagers took up hoes and scythes and spades and rakes. Someone shouted, "Even dogs jump over the wall when provoked. We are men after all!" The crowd roared, "Let's get them! It's do or die!" When the village security guards among the invaders saw their fellow villagers running full tilt at them, they turned and made off. Soon it was only a handful of township and village cadres who were holding their ground, the main body of the team having scattered to the winds.

It happened that the Huai River was at high water, and was at least a hundred yards wide. Some of the township cadres, seeing the villagers at their heels in hot pursuit, turned and dived into the river, swimming desperately toward the other shore. Others, being land ducks so to speak, had no recourse but to hide in the soybean fields nearby, or even to duck behind villagers' outhouses.

The scandalous events at Gao and Wangyang villages, where the villagers' grain stores had been ransacked and people beaten up, became known far and wide and the neighboring villagers devised ingenious ways of self-defense. Take, for instance, the people of Huangyu Township in neighboring Si County. In one of the bigger villages of the county, the people revived the old tradition of the war years when they would send signals by lighting bonfires on turrets or by trimming a tree in such a way that it serves as a signal post. In one particular village of several hundred households, the villagers devised a secret signaling system of their own: when the tax-enforcement team was seen coming from the west side of the village, the west-end villagers would beat gongs as a warning sign; if the invading team came from the east side, the east-enders would blow on the whistle. The villagers could figure out by the different signals from which end of the village the enemy was approaching. By collective agreement, at the signal each and everyone must stop whatever he is doing, arm himself, and go to the east or west end of the village as it may be and join in the defense. No one was exempt: even women in the middle of cooking must put down the rolling pin, put out the fire, pick up something to use in self-defense, and head out.

The village vet, Gao Chuanmin, was used to being asked to look at poisoned animals. Nine times out of ten, he knew at a glance that it was a case of a cadre's animal being punished for its master's transgressions. He called it "cadre disease."

A common saying among the village folks was: "Line up the cadres and shoot them all; there may be a few innocent among the dead. Line up the cadres and shoot every other one; there may be a few guilty among the living."

When we first heard of a village "anticorruption bureau" and a self-styled "bureau chief," we were intrigued. There is a state Anticorruption and Antibribery Bureau, but how could there be such a "bureau" in the village? We decided to go and take a look.

This curious anticorruption bureau was in Zhang Dayu Village, within the precincts of Wugou Township, Suixi County. This was a distant county on the northern bank of the Huai River. We took the train and then a car to the county seat of Suixi. It was close to the Chinese New Year and traffic was heavy. From Suixi County there was a bus into the villages. The bus route covered a hundred and twenty *li*, about thirty-eight miles, to reach the township of Wugou. From Wugou Township to the villages we had to walk through a flatland that stretched as far as the eye could see. Rooftops and trees with leafless branches were completely bared before us, dotting the barren landscape.

It was a godforsaken place, where the villagers barely survived with "the heavens above and the Emperor beyond." With no transportation, and no communication, the area was very backward and economically underdeveloped. But the peasants' taxes were even higher than in many other places—250 yuan per person. Take Zhangying Village, for example. This village was in fact jointly controlled by a man and his nephew, one being the Party boss and the other the village chief. These two rascals not only imposed fines at will; they monopolized the sale of seeds, fertilizers, pesticides, and other agricultural necessities, selling at higher price and lower quality. People went to the township to complain, but the township just shrugged off the problem. When the village leadership decided that every family must take part in planting 180 *mu* of mulberry, the uncle-nephew pair monopolized the supply of mulberry saplings. At over 10 fen each, how many saplings must the villagers purchase to cover one *mu* of land, and how many saplings would they need to complete the required quota of 180 *mu* of mulberry trees? None of the villagers wanted to get involved, but the Party boss laid down the rules: you can plant them or you can refuse to plant them, but you must pay your share nevertheless! Later on, the mulberry saplings all died and were only good for firewood, but even so the payment for the saplings was foisted on the villagers. In Shaoying Village, when the harvest was taken in, the villagers wanted to sell their own grain, but the uncle-nephew pair would not allow it: all the grain must be bought and sold through the village—meaning through them. The result was a loss of thousands of yuan for the peasants. The peasants of Zhangying Village had had enough. They went to the township but all they got for their trouble was hems and haws from the leadership. Wugou Township gradually sank into complete chaos. Of the twenty-nine villages within the township, twenty-two flatly refused to pay taxes or make grain contributions. Half of the cadres within the precinct had been verbally cursed or even beaten by irate villagers. So pervasive was the animosity that many cadres did not dare to show their faces in public.

It was under these circumstances that Yan Xueli emerged from Zhang Dayu Village of the same township and made a name for himself by setting up an "anticorruption bureau." Zhang Dayu Village, consisting of around three hundred people, was divided into the rear village and the front village. During the starvation of the sixties, the population of 300 had dwindled to 130 people with 970 *mu* of arable land among them. Now, after forty years, the population has grown back to 330 people, with the same amount of land. But with the encroachment of unplanned building, the land has lately shrunk to a mere 870 *mu*. There was no enterprise of any sort in the village. Except for a couple of migrant workers in the city, the villagers spent their days scratching a living from the soil. Life was hard, and it was hardest for the peasants of the rear village, where Yan Xueli came from.

Yan Xueli had been a village production-team leader from the land-reform years of the early fifties, and had kept this position for thirty-five years, only stepping down because of his age. People in the village persisted in calling him Team Leader Yan, as they had done for thirty-five years. No one remembered his full name. When we asked around in the village for Yan Xueli, no one knew whom we were talking about, until a little girl suddenly blurted out, "You are asking for Bureau Chief Yan?"

During his years as a production-team leader in the village, Yan had never taken advantage of his position to bully the people or profit personally in any way. On the contrary, he was always ready to lend a helping hand to his fellow villagers and was not afraid to speak his mind to his superiors, so people looked up to him even after he had retired from his post. Yan was disgusted with the current prevalence of corruption in official circles; much less could he tolerate the fleecing of peasants in the form of fines, taxes, and the like. As things were going from bad to worse, he decided to do something about it. "Damn it," he announced one day, "let's set up an anticorruption bureau and take a look into the finances of those sons-of-bitches."

It turned out that the secretary of the Party Committee of Wugou Township was none other than the maternal uncle of his eldest daughter-in-law. Yan Xueli figured that considering their close relationship, the Party secretary would surely support him in checking the finances of the village cadres, especially as relieving the peasants of their tax burdens was the Central Committee's top concern. Yan decided to go to the township to look up the township Party secretary, taking along with him a group of fellow villagers.

The Wugou Township Party secretary had just dealt with one group of peasants and was not exactly in the mood to entertain a visiting relative with a pack of villagers at his heels.

"Is there something I can do for you?" he asked. The group of peasants behind Yan made him uneasy.

"Of course." Yan replied, "Why else should I intrude on your highness?"

The Party secretary shot back, "So, you're here to stir up trouble, like the others?"

Yan didn't like his tone and retorted, "Do you call this stirring up trouble?"

The Party secretary asked, "So you think Wugou Township is too quiet for your taste? Needs shaking up, is that what you think?"

Yan tried to control his rising anger as he answered, "I am not here to stir up trouble. I am not trying to shake up anything. All we are hoping for is to talk to you about the peasants' burden."

The Party secretary felt as though his head would explode if he heard one more word about the peasants' burden. He demanded, "Out with it, what is it you want?"

All the peasants in Yan's group started talking about this and that, complaining of the cadres in their own village and excessive taxes.

The Party secretary controlled himself, feeling that he had to maintain the proprieties of official behavior in front of the peasants, though he was quite mad at his relative Yan for bringing in this crowd.

After hearing them out, he waved to the group, "All right, you can go back."

Yan was disappointed. "So you don't support us?" he asked.

The Party secretary had to give Yan "face" in front of so many people, so he held his tongue.* But Yan, not knowing when enough is enough, pursued the question. "The village cadres are bullying the people, and bleeding them dry. Don't you people at the township bear some responsibility?"

This was more than the Party Secretary could bear. He stood up behind his desk and ordered in a loud voice "Leave this minute!"

Yan Xueli was shocked that his relative would humiliate him in front of so many people. In his anger, he retorted, "You need not put on airs with me, you piddling township secretary. If this is your attitude, it seems that I have no choice but to set up an anticorruption bureau, and make myself bureau chief!"

"Wh-wh-what? Anticorruption bureau?" It was the Party secretary's turn to be shocked.

"Anticorruption! Antibribery! Anti–excessive taxes!" Yan Xueli stated, then turned on his heels and marched out of the room.

Word got out quickly that Yan Xueli of Zhang Dayu Village was planning to set up an anticorruption bureau, and appoint himself bureau chief. The news reached the ears of the county and city leadership. Suixi County and Huaibei soon learned about the acute situation in Wugou Township—how resistance to taxes was spreading among the villages.

The county and city leadership reviewed the situation and made a decision. It emerged that the current township administration's term of office was coming to an end and an election for a new administration would be held soon. The municipal leadership designated four capable men from their pool of talent and, hoping to rejuvenate the township leadership, recommended

* Here, in front of a crowd, Yan Xueli put the Party secretary on the spot and the latter rebuffed his demands. Each caused the other to lose "face."

them as candidates for the positions of head and deputy head of the Wugou Township administration.

To the surprise of the municipal leadership, all four of their candidates failed to win. They were foiled by a carefully planned bribery scam.

The township People's Congress comprised sixty-three delegates, who were to vote in a new township administration. Fifty-eight of these delegates had sold their votes for gifts or cash—in fact, on 145 separate occasions. Among them were the deputy Party secretary of the township Party Committee, the deputy township leader, the secretary of the township Party Disciplinary Committee, the secretary and propaganda head of the township Communist Youth League, and the heads of the township armed forces, the Party and administration General Office, the Education Committee, the township Women's Federation, the township cooperative, the Birth-Planning Committee, the township bank, the township judiciary, the township finance office, the state tax office, the trade and commerce office, the township granary, the township agricultural economic station, the township clinic, as well as other officials on the township government payroll. Among those who had used cash or gifts of wine and cigarettes to sway the delegates' votes were the chairman of the township People's Congress, the deputy township head, a delegate from the municipal People's Congress, as well as Party bosses and administrative chiefs of the villages under the township jurisdiction.

This was unheard of in the history of the People's Republic.

That so many "people's" delegates could be bought with cartons of cigarettes or bottles of wine not only was disgusting but also raised questions about the system through which they had become delegates. These delegates didn't give a hoot as to who was elected to the township leadership, it didn't make any difference in their lives.

Among the people who had bought votes to be elected into township positions, the case of a driver at the township security office was the most amazing. He was actually only a temporary worker, but by means of forty-one cartons of cigarettes and 1,600 yuan in cash, he had managed to buy enough votes to get himself elected deputy chief of the township administration!

The election scandal was the last straw, exposing the festering chaos in Wugou Township. The well-meant scheme of Huaibei leaders to replace the township's leading group with their own trusted candidates in order to deal with the problem was frustrated. When the Party secretary of Huaibei heard of the scandal, he sighed as he said, "It is high time to face the problems in Wugou squarely." Suixi County was instructed to send out a joint investigation team, and Huaibei city assembled a hundred-member support group, to help the peasants get back on their feet. The Party secretary of Huaibei joined the support group and stayed in the poorest homes, studying the situation and listening to what the peasants had to say.

How Many Official Hats Crushing Down on One Poor Battered Straw Hat?

We talked to a retired cadre of the Shucheng County Irrigation Bureau, Li Shaobai. As a young fellow in Shucheng County, Li had distinguished himself by supporting the Communist side during the civil war and had been honored with the title of "Rear Support Model."* When the People's Republic was founded, he was the first democratically chosen leader of his township within the precincts of the county. He still gets excited when harking back to those heady days of the early fifties.

* People who risked their lives to support the Communist Party during the civil war often were rewarded with such honorary titles.

At the time, there were a hundred things waiting to be taken care of, but just a handful of cadres to share the burden. Shucheng County set up offices for civil affairs, finances, education, and development, with about five people running each office. All the cadres for the county administration and the county Party Committee ate at the workplace; a few tables were enough to accommodate them all. In those times, a township administration would consist of just the head of township, a political director, a secretary, and someone to take care of finances.

With a small staff and a heavy workload, the township affairs ran very smoothly, thanks to a cheerful spirit of cooperation. When the size of the townships was enlarged in 1956, the number of officials working at the township level for the Party organization didn't change; the staff still consisted of the Party secretary and his deputy and the heads of the organization and propaganda departments. As for the other organizations, there were the heads of the Youth League, the Women's Federation, the military, and the Peasants' Association, about six or seven people altogether. On the administrative side, there was the township chief and his deputy, with a couple of committees, each with its own secretary and officers for civil affairs, finances, production, defense, security, agriculture, industry, commerce and so on, never more that six or seven people.

In a 1952 order that we came across during our investigations, the Central Committee laid down clear rules limiting the number of nonproduction officials at township level to just three. Later, when the scale of the township was enlarged, the members of newly added committees were mostly volunteers. From the 1950s to the early 1980s, staff salaries and the expense of running the township administration all came out of the county budget. The township was not empowered to create new bureaucracies or hire staff. Later on, starting in 1958, townships were by and large replaced with a new entity, the people's commune, which merged the political and administrative functions into one. The leading personnel consisted of the Party secretary, the head of the commune, some deputy functionaries, and the heads of the military, the Youth League, and the Women's Federation. Other functions were carried out by individual functionaries such as the agricultural machinery caretaker, the veterinarian, the irrigation caretaker, the promoter of agricultural techniques, the forest caretaker and others. Agricultural organization was still fairly simple under the people's communes.

When the reform of the eighties was carried into agricultural areas and people's communes were disbanded and converted into township administrations, 56,000 people's communes were transformed into 92,000 townships. Following this organizational change, the collective nature of the people's communes was rolled back. The expansion of the newly created townships added greatly to the peasants' burden. This was because by now the township had its own budget. The state allowed the townships to run their own finances. Taxes and management fees paid by enterprises, donations and funds for township projects, as well as other income from various fines and payments were now controlled by the township. This opened the door to unlimited growth of the bureaucracy and proliferation of fines, payments, and extortion under various pretexts. The trend of letting lower levels of government run their own budget grew, the guiding principle being "share power and concede interests." Gradually administrative barriers were developing between various levels of government and between different departments as government became more bureaucratized and spheres of interest developed. Those working in the proliferating government departments lost sight of the common good. Increasingly, they pursued their own interests by means of the power they held within their domain. Soon those cadres' interests were in competition with those of the people they were supposed to serve. By 1990, various ministries of the State Council alone had issued documents authorizing taxation on 149 items of agricultural products. Following in their footsteps, the lower levels of government, similarly propelled by greed, jumped on the bandwagon by increasing the number of items on which taxes and charges could be levied, expanding the scope of operations, and raising the charges for services. In addition to collecting their own taxes, the county and township would also piggy-back on the ministries' taxes and extract something for themselves on the side—called "hitching a free ride." What should have been services by the state were gradually turned over to newly created units in order to collect fees and charges.

What was the prime cause of the erosion in the gains of the peasants through the agricultural reform? None other than the monstrous growth of the bureaucracy and the metastasizing number of officials. The eighties were the period when the bureaucracy experienced the fastest growth, especially at the county and township levels, the locus of the greatest ballooning in the numbers of offices and staff.

In 1979 there were 2,279,000 people on the government payroll; by 1989 that figure had grown to 5,430,000. During this period, the number of government employees at the county and township levels increased by a factor of ten. By 1997, the figure stood at over 8 million. The increase in the number of people on the government payroll was almost the same as the number of layoffs from state enterprises: 1,250,000. The word from the top was "Streamline—growth—more streamlining—more growth," but the creation of new offices in the lower levels of the bureaucracy more than kept pace with any "streamlining" that took place at the top.

We conducted an overview of the administrative profiles of

over two hundred countries around the world, and from our study we learned that there were eight small countries that only have one administrative level, or layer. There were twenty-five countries with two levels of government: central and local. There were sixty-seven countries, including the United States of America, Japan, Canada, and Australia, with three layers of government. But our country has set up five layers of government: central (national), provincial, municipal, county, township. (In addition, a prefecture has the same status as a municipality, but manages a number of counties instead of a city. Below the township level are the villages, which are semi-official administrative units.) This plethora of administrative levels is really unique to China.

Why should something that can be done by one person or one office be spread among so many? There are many departments that do nothing for the peasants, yet they all live off the peasants. The county and townships have set up increasingly complex bureaucracies to match their counterparts at the upper levels—staffing offices dealing with industry, agriculture, commerce, education, military, financial, and youth and women's affairs. Some people say the only institution missing at county and township levels is a ministry of foreign affairs!* It goes without saying that the more temples, the more Buddhas. At township level, there were usually two to three hundred cadres, and in some bigger townships there may be a thousand. These people do not produce one cent of value or profit, but they must be paid their salaries and their bonuses, they must eat well and live well. In addition, office buildings must be put up, dorms must be provided, as well as sedans and telephones and cell phones. This would be unimaginable in the past, when a county would be equipped with a jeep or two. The famous

* A list of the offices and bureaus that function under the auspices of the central government can be found at http://en.wikipedia.org/wiki/State_Council_of_the_People's_Republic_of_China.

Party secretary of Lankao County, Jiao Yulu,* relied on a bike for his personal transportation until the day of his death in 1985.

According to figures released by the agricultural economics office of Anhui Province, Handing Township had a population of eighty thousand, but had over a thousand cadres on its payroll. If teachers were included, the figure would be doubled. Yet the township's annual income was barely 6 million yuan, not even enough to cover basic salaries. There was a township that kept thirty-five people on the payroll of its financial office—more staff than the financial bureau of a county. Another township was paying sixty-five people to work in its birth-control office.

The peasants say mockingly: "Dozens of official hats crushing one poor battered straw hat!"

In 1987, the China Finance and Economy Publishing House in Beijing published a study of the third national census. The study gave figures for the ratio of officials to commoners (peasants mostly) in Chinese history, from ancient times down to the present. The study gave these ratios of officials to commoners:

Western Han Period (206 B.C.–A.D. 8): 1 to 7,945
Eastern Han Period (A.D. 25–220): 1 to 7,464
Tang Dynasty (618–907): 1 to 2,927
Yuan Dynasty (1271–1368): 1 to 2,613
Ming Dynasty (1368–1644): 1 to 2,299
Qin Dynasty (1644–1911): 1 to 299
Modern era (1911 - present): 1 to 67

Eleven years later, in 1998, a senior assistant to the minister of finance said, "In the Han Dynasty, eight thousand people

* Jiao Yulu was a Party secretary of Lankao County, Henan Province, who was cited for his selfless dedication to working for the peasants and for his own Spartan lifestyle.

supported one official; in the Tang Dynasty three thousand people supported one official; in the Qin Dynasty one thousand people supported one official; right now we have forty people supporting one public servant."

This official's analysis was close to the figures published in 1987, the only exception being the figures for our own times: sixty-seven for the year 1987 and forty for the year 1998. This is an indication of how fast the bureaucracy has expanded in the space of eleven years. Moreover, the study was limited to "officials," and did not include teachers in rural areas. The reality is that education in rural areas is also supported by local taxes.

It is impossible to tell how many people are living off the backs of the peasants of China, but the available figures tell enough of the story to spotlight the crying need for reform of government institutions. The untenable situation of peasants forced to support a gargantuan bureaucracy and a massive army of officials will ultimately endanger the stability of Chinese society as a whole.

One Country, Two "Nations"

One spring morning in 2001, we went to the Chinese Academy of Social Sciences in Beijing to interview Lu Xueyi, a research fellow at the Social Science Institute who was noted for his work on rural China. "To deal with the problem of the peasants' excessive burden," he began by saying, "you must look beyond the countryside."

Lu pointed out that the two parallel systems for country and city, formulated during the years of the socialist planned economy, has prevailed to the present day, and the Chinese have taken for granted the disparity between urban and rural workers—"worker" being a general term for all who draw a government salary—and peasant. The government has used two different kinds of residence permits, one for city another for country, to chain the peasant to the countryside. It has also set up two systems of grain distribution: "consumer grain" for urban distribution through the market, and "agricultural grain" for the peasants' direct consumption. This system ensures that the peasants stay in the countryside and grow grain to feed the city population.* The government had also separated the population by giving a salary and social services to city workers but not to peasants. Lu said that the result of this "one country, two nations" system denies the peasants access to education, health care, health and disability insurance, retirement pensions,** and all social services, and their right to physical and social mobility. Further negatives affected are the peasants' right to engage in normal economy activities and economic rights such as exchange, distribution, employment, and fair taxation. Lu summed up the situation: "In a word, the peasant is a second-class citizen from the day of his birth. This is not a simple problem of the unfair economic burden; it is social discrimination."

Lu explained to us in detail how the government had systematically instituted policies and rules to chain the peasant to the soil: In 1953 it introduced a system of coupons and quotas for grain and oil; the peasants didn't receive any government-issued grain coupons, and so they could not survive in the city. In 1957 the government crafted a rule forbidding all work units to hire staff from the countryside. Then, in 1958, the government introduced urban residence permits. The permits were issued only to those already living in cities, so it became impossible for peasants to settle in the city with full legal rights.

---

* Tied down by residential rules, the peasants are obliged to stay in the countryside and grow grain to feed the city population.

** In principle, pension money is deducted from Chinese workers' paychecks and they are given a pension when they retire, the retirement age varying by trade, locality, and era.

These actions and others opened up a chasm between the worker in the city and the peasant in the country. The city worker was provided for from birth to death, down to cremation, while the peasant was given nothing. And, Lu added, the agricultural reform of the early eighties not only did not ameliorate the disparity, it actually widened the chasm and exacerbated the inequality. He pointed out that the current rise in urban crime could be traced to the country-city split because dissatisfied youths from the country who could not get permits to live and work in the city were the primary perpetrators of petty crime in the city. Thus, this problem could be seen as the revenge of the country against the city, the revenge of the backward areas against the developed ones. Lu deplored the fact that city people only resented the rising crime rate and rarely thought of the deeper causes behind it, refusing to face up to the inhuman and brutal system separating rural and urban, a system that has prevailed for forty years and is still in effect. He deplored the fact that so few politicians or scholars spoke up for the peasants. The peasants truly are the silent majority with no voice of their own, and they are always the first to pay the price whenever there is any social, political, or economic turmoil in the country.

The inequality in the sharing of economic resources was further reflected in inequality of representation in the National People's Congress, the country's legislative body. Professor Hu Angang of Tsinhua University in Beijing has pointed out that the distribution of seats in the National People's Congress is discriminatory of the peasant population and leaves them underrepresented: just one delegate represents 900,000 peasants in the National People's Congress, whereas in urban areas, there is one delegate for every 250,000 citizens. Not surprisingly, Beijing, Shanghai, and the other big urban centers return more delegates than the mainly rural provinces such as Anhui, Henan, Jiangxi or Heibi.

Lu Xueyi himself, as a delegate to the National People's Congress, had submitted a bill regarding the peasants' plight that contained the following rationale: "Right now the problem is not about implementing this or that policy for the peasant. It is about putting the Constitution into action. It is about giving peasants their basic rights as citizens of the state."

Who Is Being Put on a Pedestal?

The ancient waterworks at Anfeng, modestly called Anfeng Pond, in Anfeng Pond Township, were built during the so-called Spring and Autumn Period (770–476 B.C.) by Sun Shu-ao, a minister of the Shu Kingdom, now Shou County, in Anhui Province. As we stood before the lake of placid water stretching out into the distance and merging with the skyline, we were intrigued that it is called a pond. This ancient legacy of waterworks is still functioning and benefiting the area. In the township of Anfeng Pond, however, we were told of recent projects—short-lived "standard projects" supposedly the "key attractions" of the township—that were far less able to withstand the test of time than the ancient waterworks. These projects, launched during the "eliminate blind spots" campaign in the 1990s, were ordered from above.

Sun Jianjun, deputy township chief in charge of finances, winced when he recalled the campaign. It reminded people of the Great Leap Forward of the late fifties, when every village had to light a furnace to make steel. The term "eliminate," he explained, was meant to convey the absolute determination of the leadership to "eliminate" townships that did not boast of certain enterprises. At the time, the villagers had no concept of what an "enterprise" was, but orders were orders and set one up they must. Isn't this asking for the impossible, like ordering men to bear babies, the peasants wondered; isn't this like throwing the peasants' hard-earned money into the pond? "We later learned that this 'eliminate blind spots' campaign was not limited to our township, our county, or even our province," Sun Jianjun told us. The "eliminate blind spots" campaign spread to all parts of the country.

Sun Jianjun proceeded to tell us the list of "enterprises" that the township tried its hand at, in order to "eliminate" its label of being without an enterprise. First it was a rubber factory, started with an investment of almost 5 million yuan. Having no clue as to how to proceed, the villagers invited an expert over from the provincial capital, Hefei. By now, the facility's furnace is cold, the gate is closed, the buildings stand empty, the equipment cannot find a buyer, and the township is in the red for over 6 million yuan.

The next folly was a zinc-processing factory. There was no zinc to begin with, and no charcoal in the area, but the villagers put in 1.5 million, and everything disappeared before the end of the year. Since then," Sun reminisced, "we started a chemical factory, and we did produce something but it was something that nobody wanted, and two hundred thousand went into the pond without making a splash. After that it was a steel and iron mill; before the building was put up, the steel market collapsed and that was another three hundred thousand gone, like a meat bun thrown to a dog—gone in a flash with no hope of return. The county also forced the township to invest in a general appliance factory; the enterprise was listed under the county's name, but when it went down like all the rest, we were slapped with a thirty-thousand-yuan debt. Besides the above, we also had a factory to make seats for cars as well as another one making tiles. But our products were substandard, we had no buyers, and the two combined failures cost us more than three hundred thousand yuan."

"Finally," said Sun, "we started a straw-mat [plant]. We figured that we were peasants, after all, so making straw mats would be right up our alley—all we needed to do was order the peasants to grow reeds in the pond, acquire some straw-weaving equipment, and we would be fine. It turned out, however, that planting reeds was no cakewalk. It was not easy to raise quality reeds, and when we did succeed in making some mats, nobody wanted them. Our equipment, bought for four hundred thousand yuan, was flogged for barely a tenth of that sum. Altogether we were half a million yuan in the red over those reed mats.

"'Eliminating blind spots' resulted in eliminating all our savings," Sun stated. "The money was borrowed from the bank, mostly from the Agricultural Bank. The loans were negotiated by local leaders, who one by one were all promoted to greener pastures in reward for their performances. The debt is still hanging round the neck of the township," Sun said, sighing, "and ultimately the money to repay it will have to come out of the peasants' pockets."

County and township elections take place every three or four years, and cadres are moved about like horses on a merry-go-round; they cannot make long-term plans. Once installed in a new position, they all race to launch their own favorite "image project," a project to enhance the image of the county or township under their stewardship. Actually, those projects are mainly rushed through within the term of office of a particular leader, in order to enhance *his* image and provide him with political capital. So one after another, these projects are rushed through the townships, and each and every project needs funding. The bulk of the mandatory contributions toward the funding always ultimately falls on the peasants.

These ploys to curry favor with one's superior are not new. In the Qin Dynasty, the "Records of Officialdom" described a commander named Hu, who ordered his men to attack ordi-

nary peasants to boost the number of "bandits" he had eliminated, in order to build his record of achievement. In our own
era, during the Great Leap Forward, Party officials manufac-
tured similar "achievements" of harvests of "ten thousand-jin
per *mu*," for the same purpose. Their superiors were either easily fooled, or they, too, had an interest in fake achievements to
inflate their own records. Such image-boosting projects continue
to proliferate in a vicious cycle. The only ones who suffer are
the peasants, who have to pay for these games.

In Huagou Township, Huoyang County, Anhui Province, we
came across four "ten thousand" projects that typified such
foolhardiness. "Ten thousand" alludes to ten thousand *mu* of,
respectively, edible yellow lilies, grape vines, vegetables, and
households raising pigeons. Consider what a glowing achievement it would be for Chen Xiaoming, the township chief, if he
could complete these four "ten thousand" projects for the
township under his leadership. The county Party Secretary had
praised him in public, saying, "If only there were more township leaders like Chen Xiaoming!" Chen's stock was on the rise.
But the reality was a different story. Chen pursued his projects
with the same ferocity that he had exhibited as head of township security. He ordered that ten thousand square meters of
forests that lined the highway be cut down, to make way for his
"ten thousand grape vines" project. Seventy-eight peasants'
dwellings were demolished, leaving some of the residents homeless. We went to take a look at the ten thousand grape vines. Of
the young vines, which had cost anywhere from 50,000 to
60,000 yuan, only a few straggle on limply; the rest did not survive. Ten thousand cement stands, intended to support the
grape vines, now dominate the scene of devastation. As for the
ten thousand *mu* of yellow edible lilies, they have completely
disappeared. The fields have long since been turned into a com-

mon pasture; apart from that, the people did not get a single cent's worth of benefit. The ten thousand *mu* of vegetables is now planted over with wheat, with only a few patches of vegetables remaining. As to the ten thousand households who were forced to buy those pigeons, all they got for their pains were dead pigeons and empty nests. By the time we visited, the four "ten thousand" projects had already been exposed in the national press and on central TV, and Chen Xiaoming had been fired.

The township is now in debt to the tune of 880,000 yuan as a result of these projects, and the new leadership's main job is to deal with the hardships inflicted on the peasants as a consequence of those rash experiments. As for the debt, who will ultimately pay it back? The people of Huagou Township, you can be sure.

And whose image was supposed to be boosted by the image-building potential of those four "ten thousand" projects? Who was going to be put on a pedestal? Isn't it obvious? When we consider the number of officials like Chen Xiaoming running things in the vast countryside, the amount of harm that they can do is mind-boggling. By the end of the day it is impossible to tell how deeply these officials' image-enhancing projects, designed to put themselves on pedestals, have damaged the interests of the peasants.

"The Revolution Is a Dinner Party"

In 1997, the Anhui *Reference News*, a newsletter distributed internally for leading cadres, published an article on the debt problem in the countryside. The writer, Wu Zhaoren, the deputy director of the Anhui Agricultural Economic Committee, stated, "Recently a staff [member] from the provincial Peasants' Burden Relief Office and I did a survey of rural debt in the townships and villages. The results were surprising. In three townships that we visited, one owed 13 million, one owed 8 million, and the other owed more than 7 million [yuan]. Many of the [other] villages that we visited owed around 300,000 to 400,000. Distributed over households, every household would owe 2,000 yuan; distributed over individuals, every peasant would owe 300 yuan. When we approached the county heads and county Party Secretaries, they said it was not the exception but the rule."

We later learned that townships' debt burden was a longstanding problem, but it had been hidden by operating in the red and faking figures. In 1998, however, the Central Committee ordered, under the general concept of "three deductions and five reserves," that for the next three years, the peasants' payments toward various social services and funding of projects must not exceed the figure for 1997. This tied the local governments' hands in collecting more money from the peasants, and their debts were fully exposed. But by then the problem was very serious and prevalent throughout the countryside. Wu Zhaoren's article heralded the coming storm.

It is clear that throughout the country, townships and villages are deeply in debt. According to figures released by the Ministry of Agriculture on the basis of its investigations in ten provinces, the average debt of a township administration is 4 million yuan, and the average debt of a village administration is 200,000. How could this have happened? How were the debts incurred? What was the money used for? From what we learned, apart from the "standard projects" and "image-building" projects, there were even more outrageous ways of public spending.

"This is one of the effects of falsifying figures," Wu told us, "report false profits from enterprises, report nonexistent township income, and you end up having to pay taxes. In the past there was the saying 'There is no tax on bragging.' Wrong, there is a tax on bragging. You brag about your gains and inflate the figures, you pay taxes on them. After paying taxes, you are broke, you can't even pay staff salaries. Then you take out a loan."

"Another reason for the deficit" Wu continued, "is illegitimate spending, the unspecified 'other expenses' on the books. One of the abuses hidden under the item 'other' is eating and drinking at public expense. It just cannot be stopped, no matter how many rules and interdictions are handed down. Mao Zedong said, 'The revolution is not a dinner party.' Now this has been transformed into 'The revolution *is* a dinner party.' Even the often-quoted lines from one of Mao's poems—'The Red Army fears not the long march, mountains and rivers they will take in stride . . . '—has been changed to a popular saying: 'The official fears not a drinking match, ten thousand cups he will down with pride.'"

It occurred to us that the Chinese, proverbially known as a brave people who fear nothing, have now validated this claim: they have the courage to eat anything that creeps, flies, swims— anything, that is, except human flesh. Officials eating at public expense have tired of the usual delicacies of chicken, duck, fish and pork; they are familiar with turtles and have tasted wildlife in all its forms. They have passed the "test of alcohol" as their predecessors passed through and survived the "crucible of revolution." It is impossible to tell how much public money they have spent on dining, money wrung from the blood and sweat of hard-working peasants. According to figures released by the National Statistics Bureau, the yearly spending on dining at public expense in urban and rural areas is somewhere between eight hundred million and one billion yuan, enough to host four Olympic Games, to build two dams like the Three Gorges, or wipe out the disgrace of the widespread phenomenon of children being kept out of school because there are insufficient funds in the education budget.

On June 28, 1998, Su Duoxin, the owner of the Huai River

Restaurant in Pingyu Township, a suburb of Huainan, fed up with repeated failures to collect a debt owed by local officials, went to court and sued the township for unpaid bills, totaling 414,851.77 yuan. Su had gone repeatedly to the township administration to remind them that payment was long overdue on their stack of bills, but he was always sent away. Desperate, Su filed suit with the Huainan Intermediate Court. The evidence was there, the case was clear-cut, and in January 1999 the Huainan Intermediate Court ruled in favor of the prosecution. As the township was running in the red and could not pay the restaurant bills, which had accumulated, unpaid, over a period of ten years, the court ordered that the township administration give up part of its administration building to its creditor. The township was ordered to cede ten rooms on the ground floor of its administrative building, a total of about 3,600 square feet, to Su Duoxin, the restaurant owner.

The news exploded in the area. It was a huge scandal, and the Huainan Municipal Party Disciplinary Committee issued "internal warnings" to the three main officials responsible: Township Party Secretary Yang Pengshen, Township Chief Dai Jianshan, and Deputy Township Chief Chen Heping. The disciplinary measures were publicly announced. After the scandalous settlement of this latest lawsuit, people expected the leaders to control their appetites and pay their bills.

Barely one year later, however, Wang Guisong, the owner of another restaurant in town, the Royal Song Restaurant, sued the township for a quarter million in unpaid bills. To everyone's shock, the township chief named in this suit was none other than Chen Heping, the former deputy chief, one of the recipients of an "internal warning" for his previous offense. In July 2000, the Huaiman Intermediate Court again ruled in favor of the restaurant owner and ordered the township to pay up. This time the Pingyu Township appealed the decision to the provincial Anhui High Court, and introduced a curious logic to defend themselves: The restaurant was aware that eating and drinking at public expense was very demoralizing for the society as a whole, and was aware that the township government was unable to pay. Yet, with full knowledge of these circumstances, the restaurant still encouraged the township officials to eat and drink, thus demoralizing the social fabric as a whole and ultimately causing loss of public property. According to the township's logic, it was the restaurant and not they who should be punished. It was rare for a private person to sue the government, but in this case, the Anhui High Court upheld the verdict of the lower court, the Huainan Intermediate Court, and rejected the township's counteroffensive.

We visited the restaurant owner, Wang Guisong, who had won the suit. He was outside his house, happily setting off firecrackers to celebrate his victory. But we did not feel happy. We learned that it was not the first time Pingyu Township had had to exchange public property in payment for its eating and drinking debts. Previously, the Pingyu Township officials had negotiated with another restaurant owner and had traded a public building, a two-story house located on a market street, to pay for a debt of more than 100,000 yuan in restaurant bills. And we learned that the township was secretly negotiating with yet another restaurant to exchange property for forgiveness of 100,000 yuan in unpaid bills. We could foresee the only asset of the township—its administrative building—being carved up again and again to pay for cadres' eating and drinking.

The township leadership had made repeated efforts to establish rules and guidelines to rein in this eating and drinking at public expense. In 1990 they had announced that henceforth, visitors would be entertained at the office cafeteria only and that neither wine nor cigarettes would be provided. In 1994 the township limited the number of people who could be invited to join officials over dinner—three official to every guest, the price of the meal to be limited to 10 yuan per head, and each unit must pay for its own dining entertainment. In 1995 they came up with a new plan: they issued meal vouchers, which hosts and guests could use at restaurants. But the dining bills piled up as fast as the rules were made. It was a complete enigma to us. But as we made our way through more townships and counties and saw how prevalent the problem was—a problem that, apparently, no number of rules could halt—we became aware of the deeper causes of the phenomenon.

The fact of the matter is the vast countryside of China has become a gourmand's paradise. Like a cloud of locusts, officials with their appetites in tow descend on the countryside and are infinitely inventive in coming up with excuses to eat and drink: dinners for inspectors, dinners for conferences, dinners for rural poverty relief, dinners for disaster relief; dine if you can afford it, and dine if you can't; dine on credit, dine on loan; keep the dinners going from one year's end to another, from one month's end to another, from morning till night; enjoy dinners when you take office and dinners when you leave office.

A popular saying about eating and drinking at public expense runs "There's nothing to be gained by not eating since it's free; so why not eat?" To eat free has become a sign of status, an index of position. The quality of a dinner may determine whether or not a project is approved or a deal clinched, or whether a promotion is in the works. It has become a part of the political culture.

Wu Zhaoren, the deputy director of the Anhui Agricultural Economic Committee, told us a tragicomical story. A peasant from a village in Changfeng County came to their office to report the local officials' excessive eating and drinking at public expense. Wu's office passed on the message down to the next level and someone from the county administration was sent to investigate. To their surprise, the peasant returned not long after and begged them to halt the investigation. Asked why, the peasant said the investigator was now eating and drinking at public expense!

The revolution *is* a dinner party.

6

THE SEARCH
FOR A WAY OUT

The Numbers Game

Most Chinese assume that all officials manipulate figures, to the detriment of ordinary people and the advancement of their own careers. But there are some honest officials, who stick to facts and figures. We met Huang Tongwen, who was one such man.

Huang was born and bred in Huangyu, a poverty-stricken village in Huanggong Township, Changfeng County, where his ancestors had lived and died, generation after generation. Changfeng County is situated on the border where four different cities and prefectures converge, and is a godforsaken corner neglected by them all. It is situated on a stretch of highland referred to as "the tip of the Yangtze and Huai rivers." The soil is poor, and water is scarce, though Mother Nature visits yearly with floods and natural disasters. The area was designated a county in 1965, but the administrative apparatus for running a county had not yet been properly set up before the Cultural Revolution swept everything before it. Changfeng, one might say, was defective at birth and malnourished from then on. Despite its auspicious name—Changfeng means "long-lasting bounty"—that bounty had always eluded it.

Huang Tongwen's hometown was a new village that had been moved to its current site following the flood of 1954. In the deprived county of Changfeng, Huangyu was one of the poorest villages. The abject poverty of Huang Tongwen's home village had been branded on his earliest memories. He graduated from high school in 1972 and enrolled in Anhui Teacher's College. When he departed from his village to attend college, he vowed to himself that he would come back after graduation and try to do something for his native village.

In 1988, Changfeng was afflicted by an unprecedented drought, and the peasants were stricken with despair as they watched their crops wither and die. By then, Huang Tongwen was Party secretary for the county. He issued orders that all cadres must go into the countryside to assess damages, and he added the injunction not to delay, not to deny, and not to minimize damages caused by the drought. He himself also visited numerous villages and gave directions on-site, trying to control the damage as much as possible.

A senior official from the provincial leadership, flanked by Party and government heads from the provincial capital, was visiting various areas of Anhui Province. When he arrived in Changfeng, one of the counties hardest hit by the drought, he looked around and then had Huang deliver his report. Huang stated without preliminaries: "We cannot fulfill the grain sale quota for this year."

Huang's words were said coolly and calmly, but also very decisively. People in the room could not believe their ears. The concept embedded in the slogan "Man will conquer Nature" has become one of the nation's fundamental precepts. It has become customary for people to hear the resounding declaration "A bountiful harvest will follow a natural disaster." Besides, the central government had already sent down directives stipulating that the county must meet the government's grain-sale quota (the amount of grain the peasants must sell to the state at a low price fixed by the government). Exemptions would only be allowed under extreme circumstances. A drought like the one currently ravaging Changfeng was not considered "extreme" and would not qualify the county for an exemption.

Huang's reply seemed to take the inspector by surprise. He looked the young man up and down, not hiding his displeasure.

Huang was always disciplined in carrying out the orders of his superiors. He was a bright young man who knew exactly what went on in official circles: a year of natural disasters was usually transformed into a chance for "achievement" and promotion. His previous position had been a desk job with the municipal government; when he was appointed to the position of county Party secretary, he had been promoted to department level on the government official scale—the youngest official in the whole province at that level. If he was to continue to further his career, he needed to come up with achievements that would be seen as such by his superiors. But he was also a man with a conscience, an independent mind, and a sense of responsibility. He saw that Changfeng was afflicted with a disastrous drought unprecedented in the region, and that hundreds of thousands of peasants were suffering terrible losses. He felt he had no reason and no right to minimize the extent of the damage. He felt he must tell the truth.

He reiterated to the visiting official: "I must make it clear that we can't fulfill the quota. Of course I could do it. All I need to do is hold a meeting and enforce the quota of grain sales. But that would be too hard on the peasants. Come next spring they would not be able to start the planting."*

Huang said it matter-of-factly. He had grown up in the coun-

---

*Implied here is that he could force the peasants to sell their seed grain.

tryside, he knew exactly how the peasants suffered when officials fixed the numbers for their own ends and made up false reports.

After the provincial leader left in a huff, people said Huang had been a fool. The fact was, vast swaths of Anhui Province had been struck with natural disasters, but Huang was the only cadre to say that his county of Changfeng could not fulfill the grain-sale quota. It was standard procedure for officials to come up with attractive figures; good figures promoted officials and boosted their prospects. Many cadres looking for promotion couldn't wait for such a disaster to come their way so that they could be seen to overcome it, but Huang had thrown away the opportunity that had landed on his doorstep. Reports from other affected areas had all more or less minimized the damage, while here was Huang exhorting the men working under him to report its full extent. Not only that, but he dispatched his men to pester the top officials for relief, asking them to provide grain and cash, and then made sure that these reached the hands of the suffering peasants. In a word, he did everything he could to help the peasants survive the drought.

His explanation for his actions was that he was "just a country boy." He said, "Now that I am Party secretary for my own county, all I want for myself is to do something to help the peasants in my area." He studied the situation and divided the drought area into three categories: the unaffected area, where he rallied the peasants to sell their grain to the state; the lightly affected areas, where he rallied the peasants to do their best toward fulfilling the state's quota of grain sales; and, finally, the worst-affected areas, where he absolutely forbade the local cadres from squeezing the peasants and making them sell more than they could spare.

Wang Jiapei, head of the Relief Office of the provincial Civil Affairs Bureau, was a specialist in the relief of agricultural areas, and he understood all the tricks of the trade. In most cases, official reports about natural disasters would either hide or minimize the extent of the damage, with a lot of baloney thrown in about how the disaster had been fought and averted, supported with a lot of made-up figures. Later, however—once the positive publicity blitz was over—these same officials would come flocking back with inflated figures of damage to get what they could in grain and money. This had evolved into a routine: first grab the honor of overcoming the disaster, then grab relief "goods" in grain and money. The combination was a sure bet for promotion. There was even a saying, "No lies, nothing accomplished."

But now Wang Jiapei of the Relief Office discovered that the reports coming from Changfeng County were different. They reported the true state of the drought from the very beginning, and to judge by figures coming up, the disaster was unprecedented. He had never seen such a thing—an unvarnished report of a natural disaster submitted by local cadres—and it puzzled him.

In order to satisfy his curiosity, Wang Jiapei went down to the villages to see things for himself. He visited the worst-afflicted villages and saw that the reports were indeed well founded. But he also saw that because of the division into categories, the worst-afflicted villages were exempt from the mandatory sale of grain. Thus, people could see the light at the end of the tunnel, and were heartened to fight the consequences of the drought. Wang Jiapei was impressed and decided to look up the Party secretary who had had the integrity to face the truth and deal with it in an honest down-to-earth way.

"You're great!" Wang exclaimed the minute he met Huang. Indeed, just as everybody else was boasting of "a bountiful harvest after a natural disaster," it took courage to go in the opposite direction and conduct a self-invented program of "one county, three systems."

"Aren't you afraid of getting yourself into trouble?" Wang asked.

Huang Tongwen replied calmly, "I never concern myself with the irrelevant. My ancestors were peasants over untold generations. Our relatives from both sides of the family are peasants and they all come from dirt-poor regions. I know how hard it is to scratch a living from the soil. If we force the peasants to sell grain that they need, how are they going to live? How are they going to keep working the soil?" Obviously, Huang took his job very seriously; his main concern was the livelihood of the peasants.

Wang Jiapei was moved. He wrote a special report to the provincial leadership, telling them how Changfeng County had indeed experienced the worst of the drought, and how the county's Party secretary managed to stand firm and tell the truth. One of the vice governors of the province traveled personally to Changfeng County, bringing relief money with him, and thus the peasants of Changfeng survived the disaster.

Not long after that drought came the flood of 1991. To prevent floodwaters from reaching the lower reaches of the Huai River, vast areas of arable land in Changfeng were flooded—turned into watery corridors. One hundred and sixteen villages were surrounded by water; almost four thousand houses collapsed, leaving their occupants homeless. Huang Tongwen again threw himself into the relief effort, directing the cadres under him to go out into the countryside to help the flood victims. Most important, he ordered that all the inflated figures of the past be officially annulled and an accurate assessment of the area's miserable situation be reported to the higher-ups.

His colleagues at the county Party Committee became concerned that this last measure would have negative consequences for Huang Tongwen's own future. All regions are ranked on a national index system, and the index numbers for the true state of affairs would place their county in the "extreme poverty" category. Officials usually juggle with numbers and inflate figures to hide the true state of their counties, doing everything they can to prevent the "poverty" label from being attached to areas under their leadership. And yet here was Huang Tongwen once again going in the opposite direction, trying hard to get his county labeled an area of "extreme poverty." What made it even worse was that Changfeng County was part of the suburbs of greater Hefei, the provincial capital. The official story was that all the outlying counties around Hefei were well on the road to development and affluence. It would be embarrassing for the municipal leaders to be faced with a case of extreme poverty right at their doorstep. Of course Huang was perfectly aware of these implications—but he was more concerned with the condition of the peasants of Changfeng. The inflated figures would be the basis for excessive taxation. Huang wanted the true figures established so that taxes could be lifted and the peasants would get some relief and a chance to catch their breath. Huang realized that his actions would adversely affect his career, but it was clear that only when the true figures were acknowledged could Changfeng County get a chance to develop and have a future.

Just as Huang had foreseen, when the true figures were confirmed, Changfeng County was categorized as one of "extreme poverty" on the national index, and as a result received substantial subsidies and relief cash directly from the Ministry of Finances. But predictably his own career was stunted.

Later, a cadre from Jiangxi Province, Wang Taihua, was transferred to Anhui and took over as Party secretary of Hefei; he also was a member of the Anhui provincial Party Committee. He was a down-to-earth fellow, and in the space of a month he had personally visited all the outlying counties of the provincial capital. He saw in Huang Tongwen a man after his own heart. He also saw that Huang had languished for eight years working at the grass roots at the same official level without promotion. He called Huang in for a talk and suggested that Huang go back to Hefei, where he had previously worked, and become deputy chair of the municipal People's Political Consultative Conference and double as head of the United Front department for the city—honorary desk positions both. Huang had been deputy head of the United Front department eight years ago. Now, he pleaded that he was just over forty, and would like to do something more substantial than sitting at meetings of the People's Political Consultative Conference.

But even such a slender "promotion" was voted down by the provincial Party Committee, who had the last say on official promotions. The reason? According to them, after being entrusted with running Changfeng County, Huang had handed them a case of "extreme poverty!" How meritorious was that? Wang Taihua and the municipal Party Committee compromised by making Huang Tongwen head of a different committee, at the same bureaucratic level as the position he had held more than a dozen years before.

Meanwhile, Wang Taihua made more thorough investigations into conditions in Changfeng County. Finding that the terrain was harsh, the natural resources extremely poor, and the infrastructure virtually nonexistent, he realized that it was unrealistic to expect rapid development in the county. He designated April 23 as Changfeng Day, an annual event when all the leaders from the province and the municipality as well as related departments convene in Changfeng to meet with the locals, listen to their opinions, and do their best to help develop the county with cash and projects. As Party secretary of Hefei, Wang also made the decision to exempt Changfeng County from its mandatory tax payment to the provincial finance department; Changfeng's tax payment would henceforth come out of the Hefei municipal budget.

Wang Taihua ultimately became Party secretary of Anhui province; with his backing, Huang Tongwen was finally promoted to deputy Party secretary of Hefei and he served simultaneously as secretary for the municipal Party Disciplinary Committee.

Huang Tongwen, the honest truth-telling official, was finally recognized and his life changed—but it was not through the normal channels of the system.

Behind and Beyond the Glitter and the Gold

Anhui is a large and populous province, an excellent source of labor. By 2000, when the central government started the experiment in changing taxes into fees and charges, there were 10 million surplus laborers in the Anhui countryside, 40 percent of the rural labor force. Agriculture had become a losing enterprise. The peasants had toiled on the soil for untold generations and had looked on the soil as the source of life itself, but now the soil had become a burden. Thus an army of peasants turned their backs on the soil and marched into the city.

In the city, however, all the benefits of the urban residents such as the newly invented "basic insurance," "medical insurance," "housing benefits," and so on were beyond the peasants' reach. Since the "residence permit" forbade them permanent status in the city, the vast army of incoming peasants were doomed to remain migrants in the city.

According to national statistics, the number of peasants who cross provincial borders migrating from country to city accounts for almost 10 percent of the whole population. Among these, peasants from Sichuan, Anhui, Hunan, Hubei, Henan, and Guangdong provinces make up 60 percent of the total. Anhui is the source of the second-highest number of migrants.

As of 2005, the rural population of Anhui is 27 million. Seven million of these are now migrants, 1.25 million in

Shanghai alone; Anhui rurals make up one third of the migrants working in that city. This is the official number. In reality, many more migrants have found a footing in Shanghai and brought their families to join them, so that the real population of Anhui rurals in Shanghai is over 2 million.

According to a local study, the four districts in Shanghai that have seen the fastest development are Minhang, Baoshan, Jiading, and Pudong; it is no coincidence that migrants from Anhui are most concentrated in these four areas.

Anhui migrants in Shanghai have found themselves working—and excelling—in every conceivable occupation: construction, weaving, the car industry, breeding freshwater fish, to name just a few. Some of them have even been honored with titles of "Standard-bearer" or "Model Worker" in their field. For instance, a woman named Gao Yumei who works in the Tonghai cotton mill has been named a member of the Shanghai Shock Troop in the "New Long March Toward Modernization"; the migrant worker Wu Lunzhong founded the ZhongZhong Art Design Studio, one of the ten biggest in Shanghai, and capitalized at over 10 million yuan. The migrant Niu Zhuanyun is a self-educated computer specialist who works as a consultant to big corporations to fix their computer problems; he is known far and wide as the "computer doctor."

These migrants take jobs rejected by locals and make use of discarded materials to do creative things. The migrant worker Jiang Guangneng made use of furnace slag to repair roads and now owns four companies with a combined investment of more than 10 million yuan. Five hundred Anhui migrants form the cream of workers at the Jiangnan Shipbuilding Company, which builds battle ships. The chairman of the board, Chen Jinhai, praised their skill and hard work, saying that they had overtaken the regular workers in the consortium.

Some of the Anhui migrant workers in Shanghai have risen from the ranks of workers to become managers, thus creating the bizarre situation of a migrant overseeing a group of regular Shanghai workers. For instance, Tang Qizhuo has been hired by a joint Chinese-American enterprise, the Gaoshengda Fashion Company, to head a workforce of over one thousand regular Shanghai workers. He is an outstanding leader and has been instrumental in making a profit of more than $5 million for the company.

In trying to find a footing in Shanghai, the Anhui migrants have had to compete against migrants from other provinces, especially those from Wenzhou. The Anhui migrants are hardworking, resilient, and resourceful, often starting out with very little capital in the hairdressing, tailoring, repair, or fast-food business. If they have no capital, they work in construction, or walk up and down back streets and alleys salvaging reusable trash to sell for a small profit. From such humble beginnings, some of the Anhui migrants have succeeded in forming large companies. About fifty Shanghai companies capitalized at over 10 million yuan have been formed by migrants from Anhui.

In Beijing, some of the earliest among the migrants were a group of peasant women from rural Anhui who made their way to Beijing to work as household help. And then there were men who joined the workforce in Zhong Guan Cun, Beijing's "Silicon Valley." Although barely literate when they arrived, they have ended up processing computers; from being sales clerks, they end up being high-level sales representatives. They first dealt in low-priced computer parts, and now take up 60 percent of the market in CPUs in Zhong Guan Cun. Thousands of people from the rural suburbs of Hefei also migrated to Beijing to seek work in the construction business; twelve construction companies owned by such migrants are registered in Beijing. Furthermore, there are more people scattered over twenty-two different provinces, and some have joined fourteen construction companies working abroad.

Anhui migrants also have become a formidable presence in

Guangdong, China's southernmost province. In a small district of the manufacturing town of Dongwan alone, almost 11,500 migrants from Anhui are officially registered with the local security. Add to that number those that have not bothered to register, and there are at least 50,000 Anhui migrants working in that small district of that small town.

Supposing each one of the 7 million–plus migrants from Anhui create on average 50,000 yuan GDP annually, that would be 300 billion yuan per annum, which is almost equal to the annual GDP for the whole province of Anhui. This means that the totality of the value created by these migrants is equal to another Anhui outside Anhui. Then if we add up the total earnings that these migrants send home every year—at least 300 billion, more than the income generated within the whole of Anhui province—you have another Anhui outside of Anhui. Which means to say that these migrants, whether working at hard labor or at skilled jobs, are creating two other Anhuis outside Anhui.

Thus it can be said that rural migrants have promoted the economic development not only of the region they migrated to but also of the region they left. Those who leave the country are usually the brightest in the rural population; after their exposure to life in the city, they return with experience and new skills and ideas. Thus not only do they contribute to changes in the cities but they also bring positive changes back home. Take for example the Anhui prefecture of Fuyang: Right now there are seven hundred enterprises set up by migrants who returned home from the cities. They employ over 17,000 people, represent capital of over 100 million yuan; and return annual profits of over 50 million yuan. In the poor, remote villages where we visited, we often came across a high-rise building rearing up among the cottages, like a swan among chickens. Such buildings were either dwellings of the privileged local officials or the homes of those who have returned home after working as migrants in the city.

Anhui is in the process of transforming itself from a purely populous province into an affluent province, and recognizes the influence that migration can exert in realizing this goal. In Anhui, the tide of rural migration started early and the provincial government tried to promote the movement outward. The provincial departments overseeing insurance, civil affairs, public security, transportation, and construction are all involved. The provincial Party secretary, Wang Taihua, issued directives establishing that within the next five to ten years, the outsourcing of labor would be an important project, and stating that the job of the various government departments is to provide guidance, service, and management so that rural migration will proceed in an orderly manner. At the same time the provincial authorities also eliminated some of the arbitrary restrictions on rural migration.

But the benefits of peasant migration should not be overblown. In our investigations, we also saw the negative side of peasant migration. As the rural labor force drained away, local agriculture shriveled and declined, increasing the distance between the poor provinces and the affluent provinces, and discouraging investments in the poor provinces, thus creating a vicious cycle of increasing poverty and decreasing investment.

In addition, there are other problems beyond the control of the provinces, the most glaring being that migrants are not treated as equals. The cities they have migrated to are interested only in controlling the migrant population, preventing crime, and ensuring the safety of their own cities; they care nothing for the benefits brought by the migrants, and certainly not for their needs. Many places regard migrants as potential criminals and sources of unrest and leave the management of the migrant population to the public security. Thus the government has more or less stumbled into discrimination against rural migrant workers, and this will hold back China's modernization.

During the sixties, when scholars were discussing modernization, we were suffering from the three years' famine; after that, we were dragged into the Cultural Revolution, which lasted ten years. When it was announced that we were turning to reform and modernization, people did not understand that to realize the goal of modernization—especially the modernization of agriculture—it was necessary to decrease the agricultural population and transfer the surplus labor to the city. People didn't realize that this is an irreversible trend.

In the most developed country in the world, the United States, the percentage of the total population working in agriculture is just 7 percent. In Japan, economic transformation moved at an unprecedented pace after the Meiji Reform (Meiji Period: 1868–1912); during this period Japan's rural population dropped from 85 percent to 15 percent of its population. It's a similar story in Taiwan: the period of fastest development coincided with the years when the rural population dropped from 80 percent to 15 percent of the total population.

Our current population stands at 1.3 billion, of whom 900 million are rural; 500 million of these are of working age, but agriculture needs only 100 million and local township and rural enterprises can only provide jobs for several tens of millions. So, where is the rest of the 300 million to 400 million to go? Consequently, there is hope for China's modernization only if the surplus rural laborers leave the countryside and move to the city. But right now the city is not a haven for rural migrants. They are mostly homeless wanderers, and have never enjoyed equal status as citizens. Furthermore, city officials use their power against them, as seen in some of the injustices they suffer from: they work overtime for no extra pay; they are subjected to dangerous working conditions with no protection; sometimes their pay is delayed; sometimes they are robbed by swindlers; they are kicked out when they are hurt or sick or maimed. Some become beggars, prostitutes, drug dealers, or other sorts of petty criminal.

According to a study of migrants in Beijing for the year 2002 by the sociologist Li Qiang, fully one quarter of migrant workers could not collect their pay or had their pay held back; for a variety of reasons, almost 40 percent of migrant workers had at one time or another found themselves penniless in the city. Over 60 percent of migrants worked over ten hours a day; 33 percent of these worked more than twelve hours a day; and 16 percent of the last group worked over sixteen hours a day. As for health care, 40 percent of migrants had been ill at one time or another, and virtually none of them had ever been paid a penny for their medical care. Such were the conditions for migrants in the capital.

Migrant peasants have built the great cities in all their glittering glory, only to learn that wealth hardens the human heart. Migrants and city people live the same city, but there is no equality between them, no mutual friendship nor help nor respect nor civility, not even a shred of kindness or pity. The "residence registration" system has drawn a line between city and country people, creating inequality in status, opportunity, and income, and obstructing the free flow of people to the city. It has created a sense of superiority in city residents. To add insult to injury, the city government took inappropriate steps that further solidified the prejudices against migrants, treating them all as potential criminals, and they have ended up being the "untouchables" in the great city.*

*The responsibility for dealing with the migrant population (work permits, birth control, and so forth) was turned over to the public security agencies, so that they were in effect treated as potential criminals.

The atrocious living conditions and inhuman treatment suffered by the migrants working in the city have been copiously reported in the media, so much so that people's feelings have become numbed and deadened under the bombardment of depressing information. Meanwhile peasants' income has steadily declined as the country-city income gap has continued to widen. The deputy director of the Center for Development at the central government, Lu Zhiqiang, has pointed out that China is now listed among the countries where inequality of income is acute and where public resentment is running high, so much so that social stability is threatened.

In present-day China, no one wants to stay in the countryside. The peasants do all they can to leave: smart young people apply for college or get jobs through connections; at worst they flood into the city as migrants. During the eighties, township and village enterprise flourished, and one reason for this was that there was a pool of talent in the villages waiting to be tapped. The recent decline of such enterprises is largely due to the fact that those same talents have left the country for the city. The dwindling human resources soon usher in a decline in material resources, and the spirit of creativity is exhausted. This partly explains the decline of rural enterprises over the last several years. The outflow of human resources has resulted in a drying up of investment capital. According to our records, between 1985 and 1994 more than 300 billion yuan seeped away from the countryside into the city—an annual average of 30 million yuan.

It has been reported that as early as 1985, the Ministry of Public Security started drafting a new "law of residence registration" to redress the gaping hole of inequality between country and city. But that was twenty years ago, and the new law of residence registration has still not been drafted. The main reason for the inaction is the obstacles thrown up by various government ministries that are loath to give up the privileges they have acquired during the era of the state-planned economy. Their interests are threatened by shrinking the economic and civil gap between country and city. A further source of worry is the impact of ongoing economic reforms: the restructuring of state enterprises has led to swelling numbers of laid-off workers, and city authorities have created new measures to deal with the problem. They fire migrant workers to give their jobs to city residents who have been laid off, then go on to make regulations restricting or forbidding the hiring of migrants in certain trades and professions. This has caused a logjam among peasants who come to the city but can't find work, or who have lost their jobs. Their numbers are much more significant than those of the laid-off workers from state enterprises in the city.

If nothing is done to help the peasants who stay in the villages, they will have no option but to rely on scraping a living from the limited arable land. If the majority of the rural population is forced to live in this way, the gap between rural and urban incomes will continue to widen. In the end, the products of the city will cease to find a market among the rural population, and a surplus of commodities and inflation will be the result. If those in the countryside are perennially excluded from the modernization process, the younger generation of peasants will become an active element in social unrest, eventually causing a rupture between city and country that could lead to confrontation. Any such confrontation will certainly be catastrophic.

A Recurrent Affliction

By August 2002, the drive to convert taxes into fees and charges had entered its third year, and Anhui provincial leaders were very firm in implementing this policy designed to relieve the peasants' tax burden. But indiscriminate taxation and extortion reappeared like the proverbial weeds that come back to life at the first whiff of spring after a prairie fire. Still, in the year 2002, the ferocity with which taxation and extortion came roaring back took people by surprise.

Within thirteen days, from August 20 to September 1 of 2002, the *New Anhui Evening News* received 369 letters from parents accusing schools of extorting fees. The letters came from all over the province—53 letters from parents in Linquan County, 36 from Funan County, 30 from Guzhen County, 14 from Taihe County, 21 from Si County, 46 from Dingyuan County, 16 from Wangjiang County, 16 from Taihu County, 15 from Tianchang County, 19 from Guichi, a district of the city of Chizhou . . .

At the same time, letters of complaints were pouring into the provincial Price Control Bureau and they were not limited to problems in educational institutions. The province conducted an inspection of fees and charges, and discovered that in certain areas, dozens or even hundreds of items were listed for taxation. In still other areas—land control, law enforcement, civil service, electricity supply, finance, trade and industry, health care and sanitation, public security, marriage, school attendance, sale of agricultural produce—almost everything between birth and death was listed for taxation. The peasants' excessive burden was back with a vengeance. For instance, the fees and charges for building a house on one's own land had been laid down clearly in black and white and should be no more than 5 yuan, but in reality fees and charges paid—for the certificate, for management fees, for use of the land, for changing ownership, for opening up the land, for using arable land, and for construction and the like—could easily run to 1,000 yuan and in some cases up to 5,000 yuan. When peasants left the land to find work in the city, they had to pay fees for a certificate of their status; when marrying they were sometimes forced to pay for counseling. Even for public projects such as the setting up of agricultural networks, peasants were made to pay for the work.

Party Secretary Wang Taihua was roused to action when he saw this. In Qianshang County the chief of the Price Control Bureau and the head of the Education Committee were both disciplined for working together to make new rules regarding fees and charges for primary school education. The former was fired and the latter had a demerit on his record. Other cadres who were disciplined—some fired, some demoted, some getting "internal warnings" or administrative demerits—included the head of construction for Dazhuang Township in Si County, the Party secretary and head of administration for Yangxian Township in Shou County, and other Party bosses and administrative chiefs in Mengcheng, Huaiyuan, and Funan counties. The provincial government and Party committees sent out circulars publicizing some of the most offensive cases of exorbitant fees and charges and also announced that in such cases the municipal authorities with which the offending county was affiliated would be held responsible. A special bureau was established at the provincial level, and all municipal and county Party committees were ordered to set up similar offices, so that a network would be formed with direct phone lines to check and limit all cases of excessive fees and charges. The provincial authorities also called a special meeting in which they urged all departments to rally and work together to implement these decisions.

During this period, we received a number of letters from peasants whom we had interviewed, telling us that barely had they had a chance to catch their breath before cadres from county, township, and village levels were back, stretching out their hands for this fee and that charge. Some of the excuses they relied on to extort money would have been laughable if they hadn't made us cry.

In the Fengmiao Township of Lingbi County, notorious for

the Gao Village incident, excessive taxation is running rampant. Local cadres threatened the peasants, telling them not to talk to inspectors, or else . . .

We were most shocked at what happened at Wang Village in Linquan county after our report of the villagers' long and arduous road to justice. In a long letter of complaint the villagers began by saying:

> We are in the twenty-first century, China has entered a rule of law, but in Wang Village, we the villagers have no democratic rights, no property rights, no basic human rights. Our rights have been rudely violated. Continue reading and see for yourself the brutal behaviors of the Baimiao Township Party secretary, Li Xia, the head of the Civil Township Affairs Office, Zhou Zhanming, and the village Party secretary, Wang Junbin.

Wang Junbin! Wasn't he the man who took the lead in going to Beijing to seek justice, was expelled from the Party, got his name on the wanted list, and then under the supervision of the Central Committee had his Party membership restored and was elected to be village Party secretary? How could it be that the villagers were now going to Beijing again to make complaints against *him*, of all people?

The letter went on to say that apparently cadres in Wang Village are again raiding homes, ransacking grain stores, and holding back relief funds provided by the central government. When villagers made inquiries, the cadres resorted to their old trick of arresting people on trumped-up charges. The letter said that the relief funds were a demonstration of the government's concern for the peasants, and any monkeying with this fund was blocking the villagers from receiving the warmth of the Party's and the government's concern for them.

Wang Junbin's change plunged us into long and painful

thought. Could it be that our system itself is a toxic pool and whoever enters it is poisoned?

The letter reminded us of our visit to the famous village of Xiaogang in 2001. At the time, the change from taxation to fees and charges was just under way, and we went to Xiaogang Village to find out the current situation. Yan Hongchang, the head of the villagers' committee, popularly known as the village chief, met with us.

Yan told us that Xiaogang Village had made its name during the reform movement twenty years ago, when the slogan for the newly introduced contract system was "Pay in full to the state, reserve what is necessary for the collective, and the rest is yours to keep." He shook his head as he described how the latest surge in excessive taxation was taking advantage of the slogan—every excessive tax would be handed down in the name of the state or the collective. There is no way to establish a standard for what is considered "full" and what is considered "necessary." Take, for instance, the issue of raising pigs. He said: "Taxes and fees and charges are endless, and villagers gave up raising pigs. Then," he went on, "if you buy a tractor, it is not enough just to pay the management fee. The question is, are you going on the highway? Of course you are. In that case, there is the road-maintenance fee, payments for speed detection, and so on and so forth. And then, whether you farm special products or not, you must pay the tax on special products."

Yan conceded that when taxation was changed to fees and charges, some of the worst tax abuses were eliminated. "But," he warned, "a new problem arose—village income dropped dramatically." The village administration barely had any money to run village affairs on a daily basis. The township, also impoverished, hands out 3,080 yuan per annum for village finances. Village Chief Yan Hongchang counted on his fingers the various demands made on village finances. First, there were seven village cadres: the Party secretary, the chairman of the village committee, and a clerk, each pulling an annual salary of 1,800 yuan, and the remaining four were each paid 1,000 yuan. The combined figure for the modest salaries of the village cadres alone was 9,400 yuan per annum. With no money-making enterprises in the village, there was no guarantee for the cadres' salaries. Furthermore, there was no money for subsidies to family members of revolutionary martyrs and men in active service, and even less for the relief of families living in poverty. Last but not least, there were three cases of old people without families who depend on the village to survive. Each was entitled to 1,800 yuan annually, which adds up to 5,400 yuan, and there was absolutely nowhere to find the money for them. Yan concluded by telling us that there was a saying: "State finances are growing by the day, county finances are shaky, township finances are going down, and village finances are nothing to speak of."

Yan continued, "The central government and the provincial government earmarked funds to pay for the expenses of running the experiment of transferring taxation to fees and charges. Our county got two million and each individual village, big or small, got five thousand yuan. That was a great boon," Yan conceded, "but we were so short of funds that in the end, it could not cover all our needs."

Yan ended by saying that whatever the difficulties, as a village cadre he would never, ever squeeze the villagers. As for expenses incurred in the course of official business, they were entitled to a 15-yuan allowance for each official activity, but it was far from sufficient. "During the year when taxation was transferred into fees and charges," he said, "many cadres stopped carrying out their duties. In Liyuan Village, a Party secretary and a deputy village head resigned; the deputy village head and a cadre for Yangang Village left to look for work in the city. Within the last two years, I myself was reimbursed sixteen yuan to attend the celebration of a neighborhood committee in Qihe County. It's just hopeless. All I can do is take money out of my own pocket. So far I have spent more than 200 yuan for office supplies."

We were surprised and said, "Even with your annual salary of 1800 yuan, that's just 150 yuan per month—not enough to keep a family, not to mention office supplies at your own expense. How do you manage?"

Yan laughed. "By relying on my wife and my children," he said proudly. "My son and my daughter have both made good in Shenzhen, the special economic zone. My son has even become a manager at a private enterprise. My fifth child is a reporter at the provincial TV station. As for my wife, she raises chickens and hogs and makes a good return. They collectively support me in my job as village chief."

After saying good-bye, we could not help thinking that it is all very well for Yan Hongchang to run the village administration out of his own pocket, but we cannot expect all village cadres to do so, nor should the villagers be squeezed, either. Under pressure, when a campaign is on, local officials may hold back a little. But without fundamental changes in the agricultural system, without fixing all the loopholes and drawbacks in our agricultural policies, excessive taxation is bound to bounce back. If dealing with the one problem of excessive taxation is so difficult, how are we to solve the problems of raising the peasants' standard of living, modernizing agriculture, and reversing the widening gap between country and city? In the light of evidence of recurrent excessive taxation, it is clear that neither transforming taxation into fees and charges, nor technology, nor restructuring agriculture, nor any other such measures— though useful and necessary—will ever solve the problem of the peasants in a fundamental way.

The Search for a Way Out

Where, then, is the solution for China's agriculture?

What, then, is the ultimate obstacle to rural development?

How are we to restore the enthusiasm and spirit of the 1980s? How can we call forth the vast potential of the peasants in order to create China's new twenty-first-century civilization?

We talked to many specialists and looked up many studies and reports. Perhaps they all have something to contribute, and all we need to do is act on what they say.

Du Rensheng, an economist who has occupied important posts in the government and the Party, said that looking at the larger picture, it is important to create a beneficial system and a beneficial environment in order to motivate the peasants. He emphasized the importance of the system of land ownership. In the mid-nineties, the central government consolidated the land-contract system by extending it to thirty years, which gave the peasants long-term rights to use the land. But this should be protected by law. The right to use the land that has been taken out of collective ownership and is now an economic entity should be confirmed by law as private property and should be protected as private property. Du pointed out that in the past we were always saying that socialist public property is sacred and must not be violated, but now, he said, "We must point out that use of the land as a form of private property is also sacred and should not be violated." The right to land use should include all economic rights: the rights to contract, manage, use as collateral, use for investment, as well as transfer rights and so forth. According to him, all these rights should be spelled out in legal terms and clearly defined.

Another specialist, Wen Tiejun, who had been transferred from the Ministry of Agriculture to the Research Association for China's Economic Reform, where he held the position of deputy secretary-general, insisted that China must change the

patchwork way of dealing with problems in favor of a comprehensive approach to the reform of agriculture. Wen said he had
raised the question of the peasants' excessive burden as early as
1993:

> Since the days of the First Emperor of the Qin Dynasty two
> thousand years ago, the imperial rule did not reach down
> to the county. The lowest denominator of the economy,
> based on the small rural household, was self-ruling. With
> us, however, it was the opposite; the government insisted
> on taxing the two hundred million–plus peasant house-
> holds, each with its own tiny economy. For this, the town-
> ship had to set up various departments way down to the
> village. This kind of financial management costs a lot of
> money and leads to the proliferation of bureaucracy.

Wen added that the rationale for taxing the peasants is very
shaky, because the Chinese peasant had on average slightly over
1.5 acre of land per head, and there are 660 counties where this
figure is less than 1 acre—too little to sustain life, according to
the United Nations. In these sub-subsistence areas, the land is
not a means of production, and thus should not be taxed.
Looking at productivity over the previous three years, the value
of what the peasants produced was less than what they invested.
Without gain, what are we taxing them on? According to government figures the Chinese peasants have an average monthly
income of 300 yuan, while urban residents only start paying
taxes when their monthly income reaches 800 yuan. Obviously,
by this national standard there is no justification for taxing the
peasants, who are way below the 800-yuan minimum.
Furthermore, the current agricultural tax system has been in
effect for several decades, and it has not adapted to new conditions.

Wen Tiejun ended by saying that there is no panacea for the

peasant problem, but it is clear that we must push for a comprehensive reform project and create conditions for the agricultural economy to develop. It all boils down to the basic tenet that we must believe in and have confidence in the peasants and keep their interests at heart. We must have a realistic estimate of the affluence of the peasants and the extent of their burden. We must give peasants a chance to catch their breath. Otherwise the financial as well as psychological burden will be more than they can bear, and may push them over the edge.

Zhu Shouyin is a specialist in agricultural issues who completed a study called "Innovations in Agricultural Grassroots Organization and Problems in the Reform of the Taxation System." He made special studies of two important reform measures undertaken by the Communist government: The first was the decision to disband the communes and set up townships in 1985. The state set up a huge bureaucracy of townships as the lowest level of government. Related to this was the "share power and concede profits" policy, and the financial system of "separate cooking, separate eating"—in essence, a system of "contracts" between the different levels of government. These reforms, according to Zhu, created independent entities with monopolistic power that tended strongly toward the pursuit of profits.

Second, the reform in taxation first introduced in 1994, when the central government and the local governments had separate sources of income, only created confusion among the different levels of government and each level tended to squeeze the lower levels, until in the end, all hands were stretched out toward the peasants for funds. Of course, said Zhu, these negative effects had not been foreseen by the designers of the reforms, but it is obvious that without changing the larger environment within which the system works, any innovation in the system may backfire.

The president of the Chinese Association of Sociology, Lu

Xueyi,* also talked about the various problems that had surfaced after the reform. He cut through the tangle and pointed
out that the answer lies in the relation of city to country—this
bipolar city-country structure was the primary factor obstructing China's economic development, and must be changed. Of
course, Lu pointed out, changing this bipolar structure implies
more than merely eliminating the urban residence-registration
system. The latter system is linked to the structure of the division of interests between city and country. Changing the system,
Lu pointed out, would mean changing in a fundamental way
the balance of interests between city and country.

Li Changping, currently editor-in-chief of the magazine
China's Reform, attracted national attention in 2000 by writing
directly to Premier Zhu Rongji regarding the plight of the peasants when he was a county Party secretary. He shared his
thoughts with us regarding agricultural reform. The critical
measure, he said, more important than tax reform or ownership
issues, was the revolutionary reform of the county bureaucracy.
By "revolutionary reform" he meant changing the way local
bureaucracy is created and managed. The critical role of the
Party is to ensure the interest of the people by restructuring the
official system. The number of bureaucracies must be reduced
by half, as must the number of officials who rely on salaries
paid from tax revenues. People with official titles should just
step down and become ordinary citizens. There could not be
any genuine reform for agriculture without drastically changing
the bureaucracy at the county level, Li Changping stated. The
revolutionary nature of this reform lies in the fact that there will
be an acute struggle between people who are trying to effect
change, which means taking power and rights away from those
who have a vested interest in maintaining the status quo. Without this reform, said Li, the Party's directives cannot be imple-

*Lu Xueyi also heads a nongovernmental academic association.

mented. He added that if this ballooning of the bureaucracy is not halted by democratic means, we will return to an age when the transfer of power can only be effected through revolutionary violence. One of Li Changping's most famous sayings is "Let the peasants enjoy the status of a citizen; give the peasants their basic rights."

Yu Jianrong, of the Agricultural Research Center at Central China Teachers' College, did not agree with Li Changping. He argued that most of the people who enjoyed rights within the socialist economy have lost those rights as a result of the ongoing pace of reform. The only people who have expanded their privileges and increased their wealth are members of a clique of the elite. His contention is that in China today, a clearly defined citizenry with shared interests and goals in the real sense of the word does not exist. There is just a clique of the privileged and a vast number of lowly workers. There is no such thing as citizens' rights, only the capital and power and privileges of a ruling clique. Yu's conclusion: Giving peasants their rights as citizens means nothing.

Yu's solution is to rally the peasants to form their own organization and replace the current local bureaucracy by peasants' self-rule. Yu proposed that only a network of peasant organizations could truly represent the peasants' interests and needs and communicate them in an orderly way and prevent or ameliorate confrontations and conflicts. Yu added that the peasants' organizations should be formed from the bottom up and that members should be free to join or to quit.

The last person we met was the famous economics scholar Wu Jinglian. He said, "Reform can never be smooth sailing. When reform was first instituted, no one would have thought that a countercurrent against reform would surge in 1982, when the Twelfth Party Congress confirmed that the socialist planned economy would remain dominant. This was overturned in 1984 when the Third Plenary Session of the Twelfth

Party Congress passed the "Decision Regarding Reform of the Economic System." We were elated, but a few months later, inflation set in and the reform had to wind down. Then in 1986 the State Council passed a comprehensive reform program; it was on track to being implemented and everybody thought that China was on the broad road to reform . . . But a few months later, the plan was put away. In a word, we always hope for some shattering event, but now I feel that if we can make progress step by step, we should consider ourselves lucky. We cannot afford to be overly optimistic. Within the space of the last few years, so many major reform projects have been shot down again and again. Experience tells us that China's reform is going through a major upheaval."

Lately, this famous scholar and promoter of reform, who was popularly known as "Market Wu," has taken to quoting from the opening chapter of Charles Dickens's *A Tale of Two Cities* to convey his own reading of the enigma of China's reform: "'It was the best of times, it was the worst of times; it was the age of wisdom, it was the age of foolishness; it was the epoch of belief, it was the epoch of incredulity; it was the season of Light, it was the season of Darkness; it was spring of hope, it was the winter of despair; we had everything before us, we had nothing before us; we were all going direct to Heaven, we were all going direct the other way.'" Wu Jinglian ended by saying, "In a complex age of transition, we must realize that positive and negative factors exist side by side. Two kinds of future are possible. We of course hope for a good one, but the future of China can only depend on our convictions and our efforts of today."

ABOUT THE AUTHORS AND TRANSLATOR

The authors: Wu Chuntao was born in Liling, Hunan Province, in 1963. Her husband, Chen Guidi, was born in 1943 in Bengbu, Anhui Province. Both authors come from peasant families and spent their formative years in the countryside before moving to the city—Wu at the age of nine and Chen at the age of eleven.

The two writer-journalists met in 1991 when both were studying at the Writing Center of the Chinese Writers' Union in Beijing. Chen had already made his reputation as a playwright and novelist. In 2001, the couple began work on their monumental piece of literary reportage entitled *The Life of Chinese Peasants* (*Zhongguo Nongmin Diaocha*), published in English as *Will the Boat Sink the Water?*

Wu and Chen are both members of the Hefei Writer's Union. Chen, who is also a member of the Chinese Writer's Union, has been a recipient of the Lu Xun Literature Achievement Award—one of the most prestigious literary prizes in China—for his reporting on environmental conditions in the Huai River area. Several of his stories have received nationwide attention for their author's courage in investigating corruption. Both authors have received awards from the American journal *Contemporary Age* for groundbreaking reporting, and in November 2004 they were awarded the prestigious international Lettre Ulysses Award for the Art of Reportage, in Berlin, Germany, for their survey of the Chinese peasantry.

Wu Chuntao and Chen Guidi live and write in Anhui Province. They are currently working on a new exposé titled *Fighting for the Peasants in Court.*

The Translator: Zhu Hong, formerly of the Chinese Academy of Social Sciences, was a visiting professor at Boston University from 1992 to 2005. Now retired, she divides her time between China and the United States. Her previous works of translation include *A Higher Kind of Loyalty* (Pantheon), *The Chinese Western* and *The Serenity of Whiteness* (both for Ballantine Books), *The Stubborn Porridge and Other Stories of Wang Meng* (Braziller), and *Memoir of Misfortune* (Knopf). Her translations of short stories have appeared in numerous magazines and journals, including *Renditions, AGNI, The Iowa Review, The Chicago Riview, The Paris Review,* and others.

TRANSLATOR'S ACKNOWLEDGMENT

My deepest thanks to my agent, Joanne Wang. She was the driving force that linked up the publisher, the authors, and me, the translator, and made this book possible. She was always there for me with sound advice, and supported me all the way to the finish.

Thanks also to Clive Priddle and the PublicAffairs editorial staff, without whose guidance this translation would not have be satisfactorily completed.

Thanks to the Humanities Foundation and the Department of Foreign Languages and Literatures of Boston University for their support, as I struggled to work on this translation and teach full-time during my last semester.

Special thanks to Professor Joe Fewsmith of the International Program at Boston University, for his generosity in sharing with me his keen scholarship, his acute insights, and even his books. Also, thanks for the support of my colleagues at the Chinese program of the Department of Foreign Languages and Literatures: Xiaoyang Zhou, who read the original book and spent time with me in many stimulating discussions; Mingjiang Li, who was always ready to share his insights on the peasant problem when I buttonholed him in the department common room; Hsiao-chih Chang, who was so quick to elucidate points of language; and Binglin Zhao, who offered a helping hand whenever I needed it.

Thanks to my old friend Carol Susan Meuser, part of my "Rhode Island family." Through the years she found time in her crowded schedule to read my drafts and give me her opinion, and she hit the nail on the head every time.

Thanks to the "Omaha branch" of my family: my son, Difei, who would come up with the right word when it persisted in eluding me; and my daughter-in-law, Jessica, who put up with my highs and lows as I struggled through the final phase of the translation.

Last but not least, deepest thanks to Xiaohui, my "Anhui family," who read the original when it first appeared and exclaimed, "This is exactly the situation in our village, except that there is no one willing to risk his life to speak out." Xiaohui, you taught me to be humbly grateful to the peasants of China, to whom we all owe so much.

Zhu Hong
Omaha
October 2005

INDEX